Sencha Touch Cookbook

Over 100 recipes for creating HTML5-based cross-platform apps for touch devices

Ajit Kumar

BIRMINGHAM - MUMBAI

Sencha Touch Cookbook

First published: December 2011

Production Reference: 1081211

Published by Packt Publishing Ltd.
Livery Place
35 Livery Street
Birmingham B3 2PB, UK.

ISBN 978-1-84951-544-3

www.packtpub.com

Cover Image by Rakesh Shejwal (shejwal.rakesh@gmail.com)

Credits

Author

Ajit Kumar

Reviewers

Kristian Kristensen

Matthew Makai

Acquisition Editor

Usha Iyer

Development Editor

Meeta Rajani

Technical Editor

Azharuddin Sheikh

Project Coordinator

Kushal Bhardwaj

Proofreaders

Bernadette Watkins

Neha Shetty

Indexer

Hemangini Bari

Graphics

Conidon Miranda

Production Coordinator

Alwin Roy

Cover Work

Alwin Roy

About the Author

Ajit Kumar started his IT career with Honeywell, Bangalore, in embedded systems and moved on to Enterprise Business Applications (such as ERP) in his 11 years of journey. From day one, he has been a staunch supporter and promoter of open source and strongly believes that open source is the way for a liberal, diversified, and democratic setup, like India.

He dreams and continuously endeavors that the architecture, frameworks, and tools must facilitate the software development—at the speed of thought.

Ajit holds B.E. in Computer Science and Engineering from Bihar Institute of Technology and has co-founded Walking Tree, which is based out of Hyderabad, India. This is the place where he plays a role of CTO and works to fulfill his vision.

I would like to thank my wife, Priti, my sons, Pratyush and Piyush, who were very patient and supportive; my business partners, Alok and Pradeep, who, relentlessly, talk about the book; friends who always encouraged me; the reviewers and all the people behind the Sencha Touch project and other open source projects.

About the Reviewers

Kristian Kristensen is an independent software development consultant. Through his company, Whiz IT, he takes on the role of a teacher, coach, facilitator, and anything in between to help software shops improve their processes and skills. He is particularly interested in languages and the way they shape our thoughts and problem-solving abilities.

Kristian worked as a consultant for Microsoft before embarking on the journey of freelance consulting. He holds a Master's degree in software engineering from Aalborg University and currently lives in Brooklyn, NY with his wife.

Matthew Makai is a software development consultant with Excella Consulting in Arlington, Virginia. He works on application development with Python and Java using the Django, JQuery Mobile, Sencha Touch, and PhoneGap frameworks. He is interested in enhancing personal and business decisions with mobile applications and data visualization. Matthew earned his Computer Science B.S. at James Madison University, his Computer Science M.S. at Virginia Tech, and his Management of Information Technology M.S. at the University of Virginia.

Matthew writes about consulting and solutions to technical problems on his blog at `http://mmakai.com/`.

www.PacktPub.com

Support files, eBooks, discount offers and more

You might want to visit www.PacktPub.com for support files and downloads related to your book.

Did you know that Packt offers eBook versions of every book published, with PDF and ePub files available? You can upgrade to the eBook version at www.PacktPub.com and as a print book customer, you are entitled to a discount on the eBook copy. Get in touch with us at service@packtpub.com for more details.

At www.PacktPub.com, you can also read a collection of free technical articles, sign up for a range of free newsletters and receive exclusive discounts and offers on Packt books and eBooks.

http://PacktLib.PacktPub.com

Do you need instant solutions to your IT questions? PacktLib is Packt's online digital book library. Here, you can access, read and search across Packt's entire library of books.

Why Subscribe?

- ▶ Fully searchable across every book published by Packt
- ▶ Copy and paste, print and bookmark content
- ▶ On demand and accessible via web browser

Free Access for Packt account holders

If you have an account with Packt at www.PacktPub.com, you can use this to access PacktLib today and view nine entirely free books. Simply use your login credentials for immediate access.

Table of Contents

Preface

Sencha Touch is a HTML5-compliant framework for development of touch-based applications. An application written using this framework can be run—without any change—on iOS, Android, and Blackberry-based touch devices. The framework comes along with numerous built-in UI components similar to the ones that we see on different mobile platforms, nicely designed with efficient data package to work with varied client-side or server-side data sources. In addition to this, the framework also offers APIs to work with DOM and it brings in the extensibility to every aspect of it, which is a bingo combination that every enterprise looks for and expects from a framework.

What this book covers

Chapter 1, Gear up for the Journey. This chapter is all about setting up the right development environment for iOS, Android, and Blackberry. It covers the detailed step to set up the environment using which we can build and test our application, either on a browser or on an emulator or a real device. The latter half of the chapter covers the Sencha Touch APIs that can be used to detect what device our application is running, what platform the application is running, what features are offered by a platform, how to handle orientation change, and build profiles for different platforms or devices and let our application configure itself using those profiles.

Chapter 2, Catering to your Form Related Needs. This chapter covers every aspect of a form, including the different form fields offered by Sencha Touch, configuring each one of them for the user in a form, and configuring ways by which a typical form validation can be done. Fields such as Search, E-mail, DatePicker, Select, Slider, Checkbox, TextArea, FieldSet, and so on are covered in this chapter along with their detailed usage.

Chapter 3, Containers and Layouts. Containers contain one or more child items, and layouts help us position our content properly on the screen, and this chapter is all about them. It covers what are the different types of containers and layouts available with the framework and their behavior, which is a key point in developing an application where we would have nested containers, each one of them having their own layout to position their children on the screen.

Chapter 4, Building Custom Views. If the components offered by Sencha Touch is not sufficient to achieve the layout and look-n-feel that we are looking for, then custom views is the way to go. In this chapter, we cover Template, XTemplate, and DataView classes of Sencha Touch to see how to build custom views and how to handle events on it to build interactive custom views.

Chapter 5, Dealing with Data and Data Sources. This chapter is all about working with different data sources, storing data on the client side and using it in the most effective way. It shows how to work with the local data source, as well as remote data source. The chapter also covers how to associate data with different components, including form, and validating, filtering, grouping, and sorting data.

Chapter 6, Adding the Components. This chapter covers various other components of Sencha Touch such as Button, ActionSheet, List, IndexBar, NestedList, Picker, Toolbar, and so on. It demonstrates how to configure each of these components.

Chapter 7, Adding Audio/Visual Appeal. This chapter covers how to work with media—audio and video—and different graphs and charts to present our data, graphically. As charts don't come with Sencha Touch, this chapter explains the steps to configure the charts framework with Sencha Touch and then use it to build interactive charts.

Chapter 8, Taking your Application Offline. In this chapter, we will see how to detect the offline mode on a device or a platform and how to model our application to make it work even in the offline mode.

Chapter 9, Engaging Users by Responding to Events. In browsers, we have mouse events whereas a touch device raises events specific to touch actions such as tab, Double tap, drag, swipe, and so on. In this chapter, we will look at the list of touch events the framework offers and the ways to handle them to respond to those events.

Chapter 10, Increased Relevance Using Geolocation. This chapter shows how to fetch the GeoLocation information on a device/platform and work with it. We will cover various aspects such as how to find out the direction and speed at which the device is moving, and how to integrate the Geolocation information with Google map to show interesting and relevant information to the user.

What you need for this book

In order to follow this book, you would need the Sencha Touch framework and good knowledge of JavaScript and some knowledge of HTML and CSS. The following list shows the software needed:

- Sun JDK Version 1.5 or above
- Eclipse 3.3 or above
- PhoneGap 1.0.0

- ▸ Sencha Touch 1.1.0 library
- ▸ Sencha Touch Charts 1.0 library
- ▸ Android SDK
- ▸ ADT Plugin
- ▸ XCode 4
- ▸ Blackberry SDK

If you want to try out the recipes on your touch device, you may have to have one.

Who this book is for

This book is for someone who wants to learn about a framework which can be used to develop HTML5-compliant mobile applications, and can work on various different platforms— Android, iOS, and BlackBerry. This cookbook provides numerous recipes for the developers to understand Sencha Touch functionalities, in general, and use them to address practical needs in particular.

Conventions

In this book, you will find a number of styles of text that distinguish between different kinds of information. Here are some examples of these styles, and an explanation of their meaning.

Code words in text are shown as follows: "Copy `phonegap.1.0.0.js` from your PhoneGap downloaded earlier to `assets/www`."

A block of code is set as follows:

```
Ext.setup({
  onReady: function() {
    if (Ext.is.Android)
      Ext.Msg.alert("INFO", "Welcome Android user!");

    if (Ext.is.Blackberry)
      Ext.Msg.alert("INFO", "Welcome Blackberry user!");

    if (Ext.is.iPad)
      Ext.Msg.alert("INFO", "Welcome iPad user!");
  }
});
```

When we wish to draw your attention to a particular part of a code block, the relevant lines or items are set in bold:

```
layout: {
        type: 'hbox',
        direction: 'reverse'
}
```

New terms and **important words** are shown in bold. Words that you see on the screen, in menus or dialog boxes for example, appear in the text like this: " Launch Eclipse, click on the **File** menu, and select **New | Android Project**".

Warnings or important notes appear in a box like this.

Tips and tricks appear like this.

Reader feedback

Feedback from our readers is always welcome. Let us know what you think about this book—what you liked or may have disliked. Reader feedback is important for us to develop titles that you really get the most out of.

To send us general feedback, simply send an e-mail to feedback@packtpub.com, and mention the book title via the subject of your message.

If there is a book that you need and would like to see us publish, please send us a note in the **SUGGEST A TITLE** form on www.packtpub.com or e-mail suggest@packtpub.com.

If there is a topic that you have expertise in and you are interested in either writing or contributing to a book, see our author guide on www.packtpub.com/authors.

Customer support

Now that you are the proud owner of a Packt book, we have a number of things to help you to get the most from your purchase.

Downloading the example code for this book

You can download the example code files for all Packt books you have purchased from your account at `http://www.PacktPub.com`. If you purchased this book elsewhere, you can visit `http://www.PacktPub.com/support` and register to have the files e-mailed directly to you.

Errata

Although we have taken every care to ensure the accuracy of our content, mistakes do happen. If you find a mistake in one of our books—maybe a mistake in the text or the code—we would be grateful if you would report this to us. By doing so, you can save other readers from frustration and help us improve subsequent versions of this book. If you find any errata, please report them by visiting `http://www.packtpub.com/support`, selecting your book, clicking on the **errata submission form** link, and entering the details of your errata. Once your errata are verified, your submission will be accepted and the errata will be uploaded on our website, or added to any list of existing errata, under the Errata section of that title. Any existing errata can be viewed by selecting your title from `http://www.packtpub.com/support`.

Piracy

Piracy of copyright material on the Internet is an ongoing problem across all media. At Packt, we take the protection of our copyright and licenses very seriously. If you come across any illegal copies of our works, in any form, on the Internet, please provide us with the location address or website name immediately so that we can pursue a remedy.

Please contact us at `copyright@packtpub.com` with a link to the suspected pirated material.

We appreciate your help in protecting our authors, and our ability to bring you valuable content.

Questions

You can contact us at `questions@packtpub.com` if you are having a problem with any aspect of the book, and we will do our best to address it.

1
Gear up for the Journey

In this chapter, we will cover:

- ▶ Setting up the Android-based development environment
- ▶ Setting up the iOS-based development environment
- ▶ Setting up the Blackberry-based development environment
- ▶ Setting up the browser-based development environment
- ▶ Setting up the production environment
- ▶ Detecting your device
- ▶ Finding information about features that are supported in the current environment
- ▶ Initializing your application
- ▶ Letting your application configure itself using profiles
- ▶ Responding to the orientation change

Introduction

Like any other development, the first and foremost thing which is required, before we embark on our journey, is setting up the right environment so that the development, deployment, and testing becomes easy and effective. Moreover, this calls for a list of tools which are appropriate in this context. In this chapter, we will cover the topics related to setting up the environment using the right set of tools. Sencha Touch works on Android, iOS, and Blackberry platforms. For each of these platforms, we will see what steps we need to follow to set up the complete development and deployment environment. We will be packaging our Sencha Touch-based application using PhoneGap. PhoneGap is another JavaScript framework which provides the following two important capabilities:

1. The APIs needed to access the device features such as camera, address book, and so on.

2. A build mechanism for writing the code once (in the form of JS, HTML, CSS) and packaging them for different platforms such as iOS, Android, and so on.

Throughout the book, we will be using the following software:

- Sun JDK Version 1.5 or above
- Eclipse 3.3 or above
- PhoneGap 1.0.0
- Sencha Touch 1.1.0 library
- Android SDK
- ADT Plugin
- XCode 4
- Blackberry SDK

Before we get any further, you should download and install the following, which will act as a common base for all our discussions:

- Sun JDK 1.5 or above
- Eclipse 3.3 or above
- Sencha Touch 1.1.0 library

After downloading the Sencha Touch library, extract it to a folder, say `c:\sencha-touch`. When you extract the folder, you would see the folders as shown in the following screenshot:

Name	Date modified	Type	Size
docs	03-05-2011 16:42	File folder	
examples	03-05-2011 16:42	File folder	
jsbuilder	03-05-2011 16:42	File folder	
pkgs	03-05-2011 16:42	File folder	
resources	03-05-2011 16:41	File folder	
src	03-05-2011 16:42	File folder	
test	03-05-2011 16:42	File folder	
getting-started	24-03-2011 15:12	HTML Document	36 KB
index	24-03-2011 15:12	HTML Document	7 KB
license.inc	24-03-2011 15:12	INC File	1 KB
license	24-03-2011 15:12	Text Document	2 KB
release-notes	24-03-2011 15:12	HTML Document	64 KB
sencha-touch	24-03-2011 15:12	JScript Script File	366 KB
sencha-touch.jsb3	24-03-2011 15:12	JSB3 File	17 KB
sencha-touch-debug	24-03-2011 15:12	JScript Script File	745 KB
sencha-touch-debug-w-comments	24-03-2011 15:12	JScript Script File	1,478 KB

There are many files, however, which are not required for development and testing.

The docs folder contains the documentation for the library and is very handy when it comes to referring to the properties, configs, methods, and events supported by different classes. You may want to copy it to a different folder, so that you can refer to the documentation whenever needed.

Delete the files and folders which are enclosed within the rectangles as shown in the following screenshot:

Name	Date modified	Type	Size
docs	03-05-2011 16:42	File folder	
examples	03-05-2011 16:42	File folder	
jsbuilder	03-05-2011 16:42	File folder	
pkgs	03-05-2011 16:42	File folder	
resources	03-05-2011 16:41	File folder	
src	03-05-2011 16:42	File folder	
test	03-05-2011 16:42	File folder	
getting-started	24-03-2011 15:12	HTML Document	36 KB
index	24-03-2011 15:12	HTML Document	7 KB
license.inc	24-03-2011 15:12	INC File	1 KB
license	24-03-2011 15:12	Text Document	2 KB
release-notes	24-03-2011 15:12	HTML Document	64 KB
sencha-touch	24-03-2011 15:12	JScript Script File	366 KB
sencha-touch.jsb3	24-03-2011 15:12	JSB3 File	17 KB
sencha-touch-debug	24-03-2011 15:12	JScript Script File	745 KB
sencha-touch-debug-w-comments	24-03-2011 15:12	JScript Script File	1,478 KB

This prepares us to get started. As Sencha Touch is a JavaScript library, you may want to configure your Eclipse installation for JavaScript development. You may install the **Spket** plug-in and configure it for Sencha Touch development. Steps to do so are detailed on the Spket website (http://spket.com/) and hence have been excluded from this book.

Setting up the Android-based development environment

This recipe describes the detailed steps we shall follow to set up the environment for the Android-based development. The steps do not include setting up the production environment, which are detailed in a different recipe.

Getting ready

Before you begin, check that JDK is installed and the following environment variables are set correctly:

- JAVA_HOME
- PATH

How to do it...

Carry out the following steps:

1. Download and install **Android SDK** from the following URL: http://developer.android.com/sdk/index.html.

2. Download and install **Eclipse ADT Plugin** from the following URL: http://developer.android.com/sdk/eclipse-adt.html#installing.

3. Download and install **PhoneGap** from http://www.phonegap.com.

4. Launch Eclipse, click on the **File** menu, and select **New | Android Project**. Fill in the details, as shown in the following screenshot, and click on the **Finish** button:

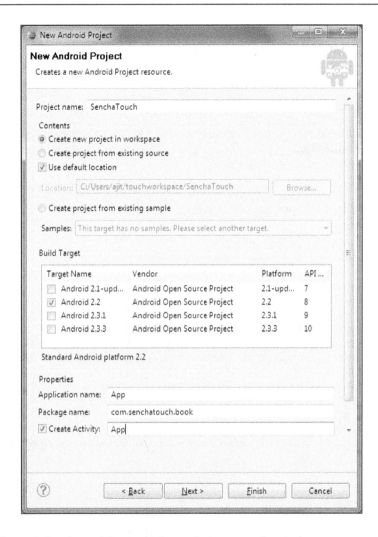

5. In the root directory of the project, create two new directories:

   ❑ `libs`: To keep the third party jar that we will be using. In this case, we will keep the PhoneGap jar in it

   ❑ `assets/www`: This is the default folder the SDK expects to contain the complete set of JS, CSS, and HTML files

6. Copy `phonegap.1.0.0.js` from your PhoneGap downloaded earlier to `assets/www`.

7. Copy `phonegap.1.0.0.jar` from your PhoneGap downloaded earlier to `libs`.

8. Copy the `xml` folder from the `Android` folder of your PhoneGap downloaded earlier to the `res` folder.

9. Make the following changes to `App.java`, found in the `src` folder in Eclipse:

   ❑ Change the class extend from `Activity` to `DroidGap`

   ❑ Replace the `setContentView()` line with `super.loadUrl("file:///android_asset/www/index.html");`

   ❑ Add `import com.phonegap.*;`

10. Right-click on the `libs` folder and select **Build Paths | Configure Build Paths**. Then, in the **Libraries** tab, add `phonegap-1.0.0.jar` to the **Project**. You may have to refresh the project (*F5*) once again.

11. Right-click on `AndroidManifest.xml` and select **Open With | Text Editor**.

12. Paste the following permissions under `versionName`:

```
<supports-screens
android:largeScreens="true"
android:normalScreens="true"
android:smallScreens="true"
android:resizeable="true"
android:anyDensity="true"
/>
<uses-permission android:name="android.permission.CAMERA" />
<uses-permission android:name="android.permission.VIBRATE" />
<uses-permission android:name="android.permission.ACCESS_COARSE_
LOCATION" />
<uses-permission android:name="android.permission.ACCESS_FINE_
LOCATION" />
<uses-permission android:name="android.permission.ACCESS_LOCATION_
EXTRA_COMMANDS" />
<uses-permission android:name="android.permission.READ_PHONE_
STATE" />
<uses-permission android:name="android.permission.INTERNET" />
<uses-permission android:name="android.permission.RECEIVE_SMS" />
<uses-permission android:name="android.permission.RECORD_AUDIO" />
<uses-permission android:name="android.permission.MODIFY_AUDIO_
SETTINGS" />
<uses-permission android:name="android.permission.READ_CONTACTS"
/>
<uses-permission android:name="android.permission.WRITE_CONTACTS"
/>
<uses-permission android:name="android.permission.WRITE_EXTERNAL_
STORAGE" />
<uses-permission android:name="android.permission.ACCESS_NETWOvRK_
STATE" />
```

13. Add `android:configChanges="orientation|keyboardHidden"` to the
    activity tag in `AndroidManifest`.

14. Move the `c:\sencha-touch` folder to the `assets/www` directory.

15. Create and open a new file named `ch01_01.js` in the `assets/www/ch01` directory.
    Paste the following code into it:

```javascript
Ext.setup({
    onReady: function() {
        Ext.Msg.alert("INFO", "Welcome to the world of Sencha
            Touch!");
    }
});
```

16. Now create and open a new file named `index.html` in the `assets/www` directory
    and paste the following code into it:

```html
<!DOCTYPE HTML>
<html>
  <head>
    <title>Yapps! - Your daily applications!</title>
    <link rel="stylesheet" href="sencha-
      touch/resources/css/sencha-touch.css" type="text/css">
    <script type="text/javascript" charset="utf-8"
      src="phonegap.1.0.0.js"></script>
    <script type="text/javascript" charset="utf-8" src="sencha-
      touch/sencha-touch-debug.js"></script>
    <script type="text/javascript" charset="utf-8"
      src="ch01/ch01_01.js"></script>
  </head>
  <body></body>
</html>
```

17. Deploy to Simulator:

❏ Right-click on the project and go to **Run As** and click on **Android Application**

❏ Eclipse will ask you to select an appropriate **AVD** (**Android Virtual Device**). If there is not one, then you will need to create it. In order to create an AVD, follow these steps:

  ❏ In Eclipse, go to **Window | Android SDK and AVD Manager**

  ❏ Select **Virtual Devices** and click on the **New** button

  ❏ Enter your virtual device details, for example, the following screenshot shows the virtual device details for the Samsung Galaxy Ace running Android 2.2:

18. Deploy to Device:

- Make sure USB debugging is enabled on your device and plug it into your system. You may enable it by going to **Settings** | **Applications** | **Development**

- Right-click on the project, go to **Run As**, and click on **Android Application**. This will launch the **Android Device Chooser** window

- Select the device and click on the **OK** button

With the preceding steps, you will be able to develop and test your application.

How it works...

In steps 1 through 3, we downloaded and installed Android SDK, its Eclipse plugin, and PhoneGap, which are required for the development of the Android-based application. The SDK contains the Android platform-specific files, an Android emulator, and various other tools required for the packaging, deployment, and running of Android-based applications. The ADT plugin for Eclipse allows us to create Android-based applications, build, test, and deploy them using Eclipse.

In step 4, we created an Android 2.2 project by using the ADT plugin.

In steps 5 through 12, we created the required folders and kept the files in those folders, and updated some of the files to make this Android project a PhoneGap-based Android project. In step 5, we created two folders: `libs` and `assets\www`. The `libs` folder is where the PhoneGap and other third party libraries (JAR files) need to be kept. In our case, we only had to put in the PhoneGap JAR file (step 7). This JAR contains the PhoneGap implementation, which takes care of packaging the application for the target device (in this case, Android). The www folder is where the complete application code needs to be kept. PhoneGap will use this folder to create the deployment package.

In step 6, we copied the PhoneGap's JavaScript file which contains the implementation of the PhoneGap APIs. You will do this if you intend to use the PhoneGap APIs in your application (for example, to get the contacts list in your application).

 For this book, this is an optional step. However, interested readers may find details about the API at the following URL: `http://docs.phonegap.com/en/1.0.0/index.html`.

In steps 8 and 9, we added the PhoneGap JAR file to our project's Build Path, so that it becomes available for the application development (and takes care of the compilation errors).

Then, in steps 10 through 13, we made changes to the manifest file to add the required application privileges, for example, access to the phone book, access to the phone status, and so on, when it is run on the Android 2.2 platform. You may learn more about the content of the manifest file and each of the elements that we added to it by referring to http://developer.android.com/guide/topics/manifest/manifest-intro.html.

In step 14, we moved the Sencha Touch library files to the www folder, so that they are included in the package. This is required to run Touch-based applications.

In step 15, we created the ch01_01.js JavaScript file, which contains the entry point for our Sencha Touch application. We have used the Ext.setup API. The important property is onReady, which is a function that Ext.setup registers to invoke as soon as the document is ready.

In step 16, we modified the index.html to include the Sencha Touch library related JavaScript: sencha-touch-debug.js and CSS file: sencha-touch.css, and our application specific JavaScript file: ch01_01.js. The sencha-touch-debug.js file is very useful during development as it contains the nicely formatted code which can be used to analyze the application errors during development. You also need to include the PhoneGap JS file, if you intend to use its APIs in your application. The order of inclusion of the JavaScript and CSS files is PhoneGap | Sencha Touch | Application specific files.

In step 17, we created an Android Virtual Device (an emulator), and deployed and tested the application on it.

Finally, in step 18 we deployed the application on a real Android 2.2 compatible device.

Setting up the iOS-based development environment

This recipe outlines the steps to set up the environment for the iOS-based (for example, iPhone, iPad, iPod) development.

Getting ready

JDK is installed and the following environment variables are set correctly:

- JAVA_HOME
- PATH

You should have created the ch01_01.js file as mentioned in the previous recipe.

How to do it...

Carry out the following steps:

1. Download and install **Xcode** from **Apple Developer Portal** (`http://developer.apple.com`). This requires you to have membership of the iOS and Mac developer programs.

2. Download the copy of `PhoneGap-1.0.0` and extract its contents. Navigate to the `iOS` directory and run the installer until completion.

3. Launch Xcode, and under the **File** menu, select **New** and then **New Project**. Name the new project `SenchaTouch`.

4. Select **PhoneGap-based Application** from the list of templates.

5. Click on the **Next** button. Fill in the **Product Name** and **Company Identifier** for your application.

6. Choose a directory in which to store your application.

7. You should see your project in Xcode 4 now. Click on the **Run** button at the top-left corner. Your build should succeed and launch in the simulator.

8. You should see an error in your simulator informing you that `index.html` was not found.

9. In order to fix this, we need to copy the `www` directory into the project. Right-click on the project in the left navigation window and click on **Show in finder**.

10. In **Finder**, you should see the `www` directory beside your project.

11. Drag the `www` folder into Xcode 4.

12. Move the `C:\sencha-touch` folder to `www`.

13. After you drag, you should see a prompt with a few options. Make sure to select **Create folder references for any added folders** and click on **Finish**.

14. Add the `ch01` folder to `www` and copy the `ch01_01.js` file, which was created in the previous recipe, inside it.

15. Open the folder named `www` and paste the following code in `index.html`:

```html
<!DOCTYPE HTML>
<html>
  <head>
    <title>Yapps! - Your daily applications!</title>
    <link rel="stylesheet" href="sencha-
      touch/resources/css/sencha-touch.css" type="text/css">
    <script type="text/javascript" charset="utf-8"
      src="phonegap.1.0.0.js"></script>
    <script type="text/javascript" charset="utf-8" src="sencha-
      touch/sencha-touch-debug.js"></script>
    <script type="text/javascript" charset="utf-8"
      src="ch01/ch01_01.js"></script>
  </head>
```

```
<body></body>
</html>
```

16. Deploy to Simulator:

   ❑ Make sure to change the **Active SDK** in the top-left menu to **Simulator+version#**

   ❑ Click on **Run** in your project window header

17. Deploy to Device:

   ❑ Open `SenchaTouch-Info.plist` and change `BundleIdentifier` to the identifier provided by Apple. If you have a developer license, then you can access and run the **Assistant** at `http://developer.apple.com/iphone/manage/overview/index.action` and register your App.

   ❑ Make sure to change the **Active SDK** in the top left menu to **Device+version#**.

   ❑ Click on **Run** in your project window header.

How it works...

In steps 1 and 2, we downloaded and installed XCode and other required tools and libraries. XCode is the IDE provided by Apple for the iOS-based application development.

In steps 3 through 6, we created a PhoneGap-based iOS project, using XCode.

In steps 7 through 14, we prepared the www folder for the application. Its contents are described in the *Setting up the Android-based development environment* recipe.

In step 15, we included the Sencha Touch related files and the application specific JS file— `ch01_01.js`—in `index.html`.

In steps 16 and 17, we deployed and tested the application in the simulator, as well as a real iOS device, such as iPhone.

See also

The recipe named *Setting up the Android-based development environment* in this chapter.

Setting up the Blackberry-based development environment

So far, we have seen how to set up the environments for Android and iOS development. This recipe walks us through the steps required to set up the environment for Blackberry-based development.

Getting ready

JDK is installed and the following environment variables are set correctly:

- ▶ JAVA_HOME
- ▶ PATH

How to do it...

Carry out the following steps:

1. Download and extract **Apache Ant** and add it to your PATH variable.
2. Download **BlackBerry WebWorks SDK** from http://na.blackberry.com/eng/developers/browserdev/widgetsdk.jsp and install to, say, C:\BBWP.
3. Open a command window and navigate to the C:\BBWP directory.
4. Type ant create -Dproject.path=C:\Touch\BlackBerry\WebWorks\book and press *Enter*.
5. Change to the newly created directory located at C:\Touch\BlackBerry\WebWorks\book.
6. Open the project.properties file in your favorite editor and change the line bbwp.dir= to bbwp.dir=C:\\BBWP.
7. Copy C:\sencha-touch to the www folder.
8. Create the ch01 folder inside www and copy ch01_01.js, which was created in the first recipe, into the ch01 folder.
9. Edit index.html and past the following code:

```
<!DOCTYPE HTML>
<html>
  <head>
    <title>Yapps! - Your daily applications!</title>
    <link rel="stylesheet" href="sencha-
      touch/resources/css/sencha-touch.css" type="text/css">
    <script type="text/javascript" charset="utf-8"
      src="phonegap.1.0.0.js"></script>
    <script type="text/javascript" charset="utf-8" src="sencha-
      touch/sencha-touch-debug.js"></script>
    <script type="text/javascript" charset="utf-8"
      src="ch01/ch01_01.js"></script>
  </head>
  <body></body>
</html>
```

11. Build the PhoneGap sample project by typing `ant build` in your command window while you are in your project's directory.

12. Deploy to Simulator:

    ❑ While in your project directory, in command prompt, type `ant load-simulator`

    ❑ Press the **BlackBerry** button on the simulator, go to downloads and you should see your app loaded there

13. Deploy to Device:

    ❑ You have to have your signing keys from RIM

    ❑ While in your project directory, in the command prompt, type `ant load-device`

    ❑ Press the **BlackBerry** button on the simulator, go to downloads and you should see your app loaded there

How it works...

In steps 1 and 2, we downloaded and installed the Blackberry SDK and PhoneGap required for Blackberry-based development.

In steps 3 through 6, we created a PhoneGap-based project for Blackberry.

In steps 7 through 9, we prepared the `www` folder by creating and copying our application specific folders and files.

In step 10, we built the project. In addition, we modified `index.html` to make it look exactly like the one created in the *Setting up the Android-based development environment* recipe.

In steps 11 and 12, we deployed and tested the application in the simulator, as well as in the real Blackberry device.

See also

The recipe named *Setting up the Android-based development environment* in this chapter.

Setting up the browser-based development environment

In the previous recipes, we saw how we can make use of PhoneGap to build, package, and deploy the Sencha Touch applications directly on the device. Another very popular kind of application is the browser-based one. All the devices which Sencha Touch supports come along with Internet browsers. In this recipe, we will see how we can develop a Sencha Touch application, access it, and test it using Internet browsers.

Sencha Touch is moving towards using HTML5 features but, today, it heavily uses the WebKit engine and, hence, in order to test the applications, we will require a browser which runs on the WebKit engine—Opera, Safari, and Chrome. We can also test most of the things on a browser running on your desktop/workstation (except things such as orientation changes).

[Sencha Touch applications do not work on browsers using the Gecko engine, which includes Mozilla Firefox.]

We will be using this environment for this book to demonstrate the capabilities of Sencha Touch.

Getting ready

Make sure that your device has a WebKit compatible browser—Opera, Safari, or Chrome.

Verify that you have your GPRS or Wi-Fi enabled and working on your device, so that you are able to access the Internet.

You should have a web server such as Apache or Nginx deployed on a server, which is accessible on the Internet. For example, I have my web server running on `http://walkingtree.in`.

How to do it...

Carry out the following steps:

1. Create a folder named `touch` in your web server's `deployment/root` folder, for example, `public_html` or `htdocs`.

2. Copy the content of the `assets\www` folder, prepared in the *Setting up the Android-based development environment* recipe, to the `touch` folder. After copying, the `touch` folder should have the following files:

3. Remove `phonegap-1.0.0.js` from `index.html`.

4. Go to the Internet browser on your device and enter the URL: `http://<your domain or ip address>:<port>/touch` (for example, `http://walkingtree.in/touch`) in the address bar and hit **Go**. You should have the application running inside the browser.

How it works...

In step 1, we created the `touch` folder as a placeholder to keep our application code inside it. This would help us avoid polluting the web server's `root` folder.

In step 2, we copied the contents from the `assets\www` folder, which we prepared in the *Setting up the Android-based development environment* recipe. In step 3, we removed the `<script>` tag including the PhoneGap JS file, as we are not going to use its APIs in this book. Finally, in step 4, we accessed the application from a browser.

See also

The recipe named *Setting up the Android-based development environment* in this chapter.

Setting up the production environment

This recipe describes the steps required to create a production-ready package of the application. These steps are mentioned for the Sencha Touch-related applications; however, they can also be applied to any JavaScript-based application.

Getting ready

Make sure that you have completed the steps outlined in the *Setting up the browser-based development environment* recipe.

How to do it...

Carry out the following steps:

1. Trim down the Sencha Touch library by deleting the files and folders which are not required in the production environment. The following screenshot shows the files and folders which should be deleted from the `sencha-touch` folder:

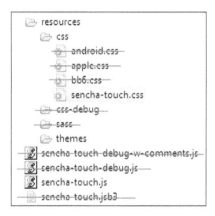

2. Update the `index.html` file to include `sencha-touch.js` in place of `sencha-touch-debug.js`.

3. Merge and minify your JavaScripts and CSS files. You may use the tool of your choice. Say you have created `yapps-all.js` (for now, it contains only the `ch01_01.js`) and `yapps-all.css` (this may contain the merged `sencha-touch.css` and any of our application-specific CSS file, say, `yapps.css`) as the merged and minified JavaScripts and CSS files, respectively.

 Sencha uses and recommends **JSBuilder** and **YUI Compressor** and you can read more about this at the following URL: http://www.sencha.com/products/jsbuilder.

4. Remove the inclusion of the individual application-specific JavaScript files and CSS files from `index.html`.

5. Include `yapps-all.js` and `yapps-all.css`.

6. Deploy the application on your production server.

How it works...

In step 1, we removed the unwanted folders and files which are not required for a typical production deployment.

In step 2, we replaced the debug version of the library with the production ready version, which is a compressed and minified version of the debug version. This file will not have the comments and also the code is obfuscated.

In step 3, we merged all the JS/CSS files into one single file and minified them. You may want to find out the best way to combine the files. This is generally done to load the application quickly. You may choose to combine one or more files into one or create individual minified files. It is totally based on your project design and code structure.

In steps 4 and 5, we removed the individual inclusion of the JS and CSS files from `index.html` and included the merged and minified ones. This recipe does not show the PhoneGap-related JS file. However, if your application is using it, then make sure that you also minify it, as the default one is not the production ready file.

See also

- The recipe named *Setting up the browser-based development environment* in this chapter
- The recipe named *Setting up the Android-based development environment* in this chapter

Detecting the device

Different devices offer different capabilities and hence for an application developer, it becomes important to identify the exact device, so that it can respond to the events in the most appropriate way. This recipe describes how we can detect the device on which the application is being run.

How to do it...

Carry out the following steps:

1. Create and open a new file `ch01_02.js` in the `ch01` folder and paste the following code into it:

```
Ext.setup({
  onReady: function() {
    if (Ext.is.Android)
      Ext.Msg.alert("INFO", "Welcome Android user!");
```

```
    if (Ext.is.Blackberry)
      Ext.Msg.alert("INFO", "Welcome Blackberry user!");

    if (Ext.is.iPad)
      Ext.Msg.alert("INFO", "Welcome iPad user!");
  }
});
```

2. Remove the following line from `index.html`:

```
<script type="text/javascript" charset="utf-8"
  src="ch01/ch01_01.js"></script>
```

3. Include the following line in `index.html`:

```
<script type="text/javascript" charset="utf-8"
  src="ch01/ch01_02.js"></script>
```

4. Deploy and run the application. Based on the device on which the application is being run, you will see a corresponding message.

How it works...

The `Ext.is` class is instrumental in detecting the target device on which your application is being run. It uses the JavaScript's `navigator` object to detect the browser details, including the platform/device. For example, if the `platform` property in the `navigator` object has `iPhone` in it, then the target platform is iPhone, whereas if the `userAgent` property in the `navigator` object has `Android`, then the platform is Android.

See also

▸ The recipe named *Setting up the browser-based development environment* in this chapter

▸ The recipe named *Setting up the production environment* in this chapter

Finding information about features that are supported in the current environment

Each device and platform offers a rich set of functionality. However, it is difficult to identify a set of features which are available across devices and platforms. In addition, even if we happen to find out the list of common features, there may be reasons where you may want to use a feature on a device which is not present on other devices and you would make your application work on those devices by performing the best approximation of that specific feature. For example, on a device if SVG is supported, you may want to make use of that feature in your application to render images using it, so that they are scalable. However, if another device does not support SVG, you may want to fall back to rendering your image into JPEG/PNG, so that the image will be visible to the user. This recipe describes how an application can detect the different features that a device supports. This comes in very handy to enable/disable certain application features based on the device-supported features.

How to do it...

Carry out the following steps:

1. Create and open a new file named `ch01_03.js` in the `ch01` folder and paste the following code into it:

```
Ext.setup({
  onReady: function() {
    var supportedFeatures = "Ext.supports.AudioTag : " +
      (Ext.supports.AudioTag ? "On" : "Off");
    supportedFeatures += "\nExt.supports.CSS3BorderRadius : " +
      (Ext.supports.CSS3BorderRadius ? "On" : "Off");
    supportedFeatures += "\nExt.supports.CSS3DTransform : " +
      (Ext.supports.CSS3DTransform ? "On" : "Off");
    supportedFeatures += "\nExt.supports.CSS3LinearGradient : " +
      (Ext.supports.CSS3LinearGradient ? "On" : "Off");
    supportedFeatures += "\nExt.supports.Canvas : " +
      (Ext.supports.Canvas ? "On" : "Off");
    supportedFeatures += "\nExt.supports.DeviceMotion : " +
      (Ext.supports.DeviceMotion ? "On" : "Off");
    supportedFeatures += "\nExt.supports.Float : " +
      (Ext.supports.Float ? "On" : "Off");
    supportedFeatures += "\nExt.supports.GeoLocation : " +
      (Ext.supports.GeoLocation ? "On" : "Off");
    supportedFeatures += "\nExt.supports.History : " +
      (Ext.supports.History ? "On" : "Off");
    supportedFeatures += "\nExt.supports.OrientationChange : " +
      (Ext.supports.OrientationChange ? "On" : "Off");
```

```
supportedFeatures += "\nExt.supports.RightMargin : " +
    (Ext.supports.RightMargin ? "On" : "Off");
supportedFeatures += "\nExt.supports.SVG : " +
    (Ext.supports.SVG ? "On" : "Off");
supportedFeatures += "\nExt.supports.Touch : " +
    (Ext.supports.Touch ? "On" : "Off");
supportedFeatures += "\nExt.supports.Transitions : " +
    (Ext.supports.Transitions ? "On" : "Off");
supportedFeatures += "\nExt.supports.TransparentColor : " +
    (Ext.supports.TransparentColor ? "On" : "Off");
supportedFeatures += "\nExt.supports.VML : " +
    (Ext.supports.VML ? "On" : "Off");

    Ext.Msg.alert("INFO", supportedFeatures);
    }
});
```

2. Remove the following line from `index.html`:

```
<script type="text/javascript" charset="utf-8"
    src="ch01/ch01_02.js"></script>
```

3. Include the following line in `index.html`:

```
<script type="text/javascript" charset="utf-8"
    src="ch01/ch01_03.js"></script>
```

4. Deploy and run the application.

How it works...

Check that the support for different features is encapsulated inside the Sencha Touch's `Ext.supports` class. This class applies different mechanisms to find out whether a requested feature is supported by the target platform/device. For example, to find out whether the device supports touch, this class checks whether `ontouchstart` is present in the `window` object. Another example is, to find out whether SVG is supported on the target platform, it tries to add an SVG element (which it removes after successful creation and setting the flag to indicate that the device supports SVG) to the `document`.

See also

- ▶ The recipe named *Setting up the browser-based development environment* in this chapter

- ▶ The recipe named *Setting up the production environment* in this chapter

Initializing your application

So far, we have been using `Ext.setup` to enter into our application, where the entry point is provided by the `onReady` method, which is invoked when the document is ready. However, in an enterprise setup, an application is much more complex and needs more configurations that that which `Ext.setup` provides. For example, if you would like to configure your application with the history support, rather than doing it for individual pages or components, you may like your application to configure it based on the target platform and many more. These kinds of needs are addressed by Sencha Touch by providing a dedicated class.

Sencha Touch provides an `Ext.Application` class to create an application. This is a convenient way to create an application. Besides configuring your application, this class also allows you to structure your complete application in the form of Model-View-Controller and initialize it using a convenient method. The class allows the user to implement a function, which can be called when the application is launched. In this recipe, we will see how to create and initialize an application using the `Ext.Application` class.

How to do it...

Carry out the following steps:

1. Create and open a new file `ch01_04.js` in the `ch01` folder and paste the following code into it:

```
new Ext.Application({
  name: 'MyApp',

  launch: function() {
    this.viewport = new Ext.Panel({
      fullscreen: true,
      items : [
        {
            html: 'Welcome to My App!'
        }
      ]
    });
  }
});
```

2. Remove the following line from `index.html`:

```
<script type="text/javascript" charset="utf-8"
  src="ch01/ch01_03.js"></script>
```

3. Include the following line in `index.html`:

```
<script type="text/javascript" charset="utf-8"
    src="ch01/ch01_04.js"></script>
```

4. Deploy and run the application.

How it works...

`Ext.Application` provides various configuration options, which can be specified while constructing the `Application` instance. The `name` property provides the application name, which is also used as the namespace for the application being initialized. In addition, by default, the following namespaces are registered using the `name` property value:

- ▶ `MyApp.models`
- ▶ `MyApp.views`
- ▶ `MyApp.controllers`
- ▶ `MyApp.stores`

Another property is `launch`. The `launch` function creates the application's viewport and runs any actions the application needs to perform when it boots up. The `launch` function is run once. In the preceding code, we are creating a panel in the full screen mode which will show **Welcome to My App!** in its body.

 If you are using PhoneGap, aviod using the `app` and `phonegap` namespaces, as they are used by PhoneGap and usage of them may throw up errors.

See also

The recipe named *Setting up browser-based development environment* in this chapter.

Tweaking your application to configure itself using profiles

This recipe describes how you can set up multiple profiles for your application and let your application configure itself using the profile.

How to do it...

Carry out the following steps:

1. Create and open a new file named `ch01_05.js` in the `ch01` folder and paste the following code into it:

```
new Ext.Application({
  name: 'MyApp',
  profiles: {
    phoneBlackberry: function() {
      return Ext.is.Blackberry;
    },
    phoneAndroid: function() {
      return Ext.is.Android;
    },
    tabletPortrait: function() {
      return Ext.is.Tablet && Ext.orientation == 'portrait';
    },
    tabletLandscape: function() {
      return Ext.is.Tablet && Ext.orientation == 'landscape';
    }
  },
  launch: function() {
    this.viewport = new Ext.Panel({
      fullscreen: true,
      items : [
        {
          html: 'Welcome to My App!' + ' - profile - ' +
            this.getProfile(),

        }
      ]
    });
  }

});
```

2. Remove the following line from `index.html`:

```
<script type="text/javascript" charset="utf-8"
  src="ch01/ch01_04.js"></script>
```

3. Include the following line in `index.html`:

```
<script type="text/javascript" charset="utf-8"
    src="ch01/ch01_05.js"></script>
```

4. Deploy and run the application.

How it works...

The `Application` class provides a property named `profiles`, which is used to set up multiple profiles, as shown in the preceding code. When the application is launched, each of the configured profile functions such as `phoneBlackberry`, `phoneAndroid`, and so on, is evaluated in the order of their definition. The first profile function that returns true is the one which becomes the profile of the application. For example, if we are running the application on the Android phone, then `phoneAndroid` is the first function that will return true and, hence, the profile of the application will be set to `phoneAndroid`.

The current profile can be fetched from the application or any component. You can use the `getProfile()` method which returns the name of the profile, for example, `phoneAndroid`.

The profile is applied, by default, at the time of the application launch.

There's more...

There are few more interesting options and features that the `Application` class provides to have a better control of the profiles and their application. Let's see what else can be done with the profiles.

Do not apply the profile at the time of application launch

As we saw, the profile is applied to the components at the time of application launch. It may not be desirable all the time. You may want to apply the profiles at a later stage in your application. For example, your application has a photo viewer which shows the photo on the left-hand side and the photo detail on the right-hand side of the page. Moreover, due to the layout, and to have a better view of the photo and its detail, say, you always want the user to switch to the landscape mode. In this case, you would like to wait until the user opens the viewer and that is when you would like to identify the profile and take action accordingly.

Applying the profile at the application launch time is controlled by the `setProfilesOnLaunch` property. By default, this is set to `true`. In your application initialization, you should pass the following additional config:

```
setProfilesOnLaunch : false
```

Therefore, the code would look something like this:

```
new Ext.Application({
    name: 'MyApp',
    setProfilesOnLaunch: false,
    profiles: {
....
```

Do not apply the profile on the components, by default

By default, at the launch time, the current profile is applied to all the components of the application. If you do not want this to happen, then you will have to set `autoUpdateComponentProfiles` to `false` during your application initialization.

Ignoring the profile change

In some applications, you may want to ignore the effect of profile changes. To do so, we will have to implement the handler for the `beforeprofilechange` event and return `false` from it. The `Application` class raises this event after it has detected the profile change and before it would start to apply the profile to the components. If `false` is returned from the handler, it would not apply the profile to the components. The following code snippet shows how the handler needs to be written:

```
new Ext.Application({
    name: 'MyApp',
    setProfilesOnLaunch: false,
    profiles: {
....
    },
    beforeprofilechange: function(profile, oldProfile) {
      return false;
    }
```

Deferred application of profile

If you choose not to apply the profile at the time of launch, but defer it until the event of interest occurs, then you can achieve this by calling the `determineProfile()` method of the `Application` class. In addition, you will have to make sure that `autoUpdateComponentProfiles` is set to `true` before the method is called.

See also

▶ The recipe named *Setting up the browser-based development environment* in this chapter

▶ The recipe named *Initializing your application* in this chapter

Responding to the orientation change

It is possible to change the orientation from portrait to landscape mode by turning your device. Many applications make use of this facility to provide better usability to the user. For example, when we are working with the virtual keyboard and change the orientation from portrait to landscape, the keyboard gets bigger and it becomes easier to type. Most of the devices support orientation changes and, based on your application, you may want to make use of this feature to change your application layout or behavior. Sencha Touch automatically watches for this and notifies all the application components by sending them the `orientationchange` event. If the application or any component of it needs to change its behavior, then the corresponding component registers a handler for the `orientationchange` event.

How to do it...

Carry out the following steps:

1. Create and open a new file named `ch01_06.js` in the `ch01` folder and paste the following code into it:

```
new Ext.Application({
  name: 'MyApp',

  profiles: {
    phoneBlackberry: function() {
      return Ext.is.Blackberry;
    },
    phoneAndroid: function() {
      return Ext.is.Android;
    },
    tabletPortrait: function() {
      return Ext.is.Tablet && Ext.orientation == 'portrait';
    },
    tabletLandscape: function() {
      return Ext.is.Tablet && Ext.orientation == 'landscape';
    }
  },
  launch: function() {
```

```
      this.viewport = new Ext.Panel({
        fullscreen: true,
        listeners: {
          orientationchange : function( thisPnl, orientation,
          width, height ){
             Ext.Msg.alert("INFO","Orientation: " + orientation
             + " : width:" + width + ":height:" + height);
          }
        },
        items : [
        {
          html: 'Welcome to My App!' + ' - profile - ' +
            this.getProfile(),
        }
        ]
      });
    }

  });
```

2. Remove the following line from `index.html`:

    ```
    <script type="text/javascript" charset="utf-8"
      src="ch01/ch01_05.js"></script>
    ```

3. Include the following line in `index.html`:

    ```
    <script type="text/javascript" charset="utf-8"
      src="ch01/ch01_06.js"></script>
    ```

4. Deploy and run the application.

How it works...

The Sencha Touch framework provides certain properties on the components, which directly affect the orientation change detection and notification. There are certain properties on the components based on which it derives whether the orientation change needs to be notified. The `monitorOrientation` property on the component directly instructs the library whether it has to monitor for the orientation change. This property is, by default, set to `false`—meaning, do not monitor for the orientation change. Hence, `beforeorientationchange` and `orientationchange` events will not be fired. However, the property `fullscreen` affects the `monitorOrientation` value. In the preceding code, `fullscreen` has been set to `true`, which sets the `monitorOrientation` to `true` and due to this, the library will monitor for the orientation change. When that happens, it fires the `beforeorientationchange` and `orientationchange` events. Any component which intends to handle the orientation change must implement the handler for these events.

On the container components (for example, Panel, TabPanel, and so on) enabling scrolling immediately sets the `monitorOrientation` to `true`.

There's more...

Say, in your application, monitoring of the orientation change has been enabled, but some components neither want to handle the orientation change-related events, nor do they want the default behavior to be executed. In this case, these components will have to stop the orientation change and the subsequent section shows how to achieve that.

Stopping the orientation change

If a component wants to ignore the orientation change, then it should implement the `beforeorientationchange` listener which should return `false`. The following code snippet shows how to do it:

```
beforeorientationchange: function(thisPnl, orientation, width, height)
{
    return false;
}
```

See also

- ▶ The recipe named *Setting up the browser-based development environment* in this chapter
- ▶ The recipe named *Initializing your application* in this chapter

2
Catering to your Form Related Needs

In this chapter, we will cover:

- ▶ Getting your form ready with FormPanel
- ▶ Working with search
- ▶ Putting custom validation in the e-mail field
- ▶ Working with dates using DatePicker
- ▶ Making a field hidden
- ▶ Working with the select field
- ▶ Changing the value using Slider
- ▶ Spinning the number wheel using Spinner
- ▶ Toggling between your two choices
- ▶ Checkbox and checkbox group
- ▶ Text and TextArea
- ▶ Grouping fields with FieldSet
- ▶ Validating your form

Introduction

Most of the useful applications not only present the data, but also accept inputs from their users. When we think of having a way to accept inputs from the user, send them to the server for further processing, and allow the user to modify them, we think of forms and the form fields. If our application requires users to enter some information, then we go about using the HTML form fields, such as `<input>`, `<select>`, and so on, and wrap inside a `<form>` element. Sencha Touch uses these tags and provides convenient JavaScript classes to work with the form and its fields. It provides field classes such as `Url`, `Toggle`, `Select`, `Text`, and so on. Each of these classes provides properties to initialize the field, handle the events, and utility methods to manipulate the behavior and the values of the field. On the other side, the form takes care of the rendering of the fields and also handles the data submission.

Each field can be created by using the JSON notation (**JavaScript Object Notation**—http://www.json.org) or by creating an instance of the class. For example, a text field can either be constructed by using the following JSON notation:

```
{
  xtype: 'textfield',
  name: 'text',
  label: 'My Text'
}
```

Alternatively, we can use the following class constructor:

```
var txtField = new Ext.form.Text({
  name: 'text',
  label: 'My Text'
});
```

The first approach relies on `xtype`, which is a type assigned to each of the Sencha Touch components. It is used as shorthand for the class. The basic difference between the two is that the `xtype` approach is more for the lazy initialization and rendering. The object is created only when it is required. In any application, we would use a combination of these two approaches.

In this chapter, we will go through all the form fields and understand how to make use of them and learn about their specific behaviors. In addition, we will see how to create a form using one or more form fields and handle the form validation and submission.

Getting your form ready with FormPanel

This recipe shows how to create a basic form using Sencha Touch and implement some of the behaviors such as submitting the form data, handling errors during the submission, and so on.

Getting ready

Make sure that you have set up your development environment by following the recipes outlined in *Chapter 1, Gear up for the Journey*.

How to do it...

Carry out the following steps:

1. Create a `ch02` folder in the same folder where we had created the `ch01` folder.

2. Create and open a new file named `ch02_01.js` and paste the following code into it:

```
Ext.setup({
  onReady: function() {

    var form;

    //form and related fields config
    var formBase = {
      //enable vertical scrolling in case the form exceeds the
        page height
      scroll: 'vertical',
      url: 'http://localhost/test.php',
      items: [{//add a fieldset
        xtype: 'fieldset',
        title: 'Personal Info',
        instructions: 'Please enter the information above.',
        //apply the common settings to all the child items
          of the fieldset
        defaults: {
          required: true,     //required field
          labelAlign: 'left',
          labelWidth: '40%'
        },
        items: [
          {//add a text field
            xtype: 'textfield',
            name : 'name',
```

```
              label: 'Name',
              useClearIcon: true,//shows the clear icon in the
                 field when user types
              autoCapitalize : false
          }, {//add a password field
            xtype: 'passwordfield',
            name : 'password',
            label: 'Password',
            useClearIcon: false
          }, {
            xtype: 'passwordfield',
            name : 'reenter',
            label: 'Re-enter Password',
            useClearIcon: true
          }, {//add an email field
            xtype: 'emailfield',
            name : 'email',
            label: 'Email',
            placeHolder: 'you@sencha.com',
            useClearIcon: true
          }]
      }
    ],
    listeners : {
      //listener if the form is submitted, successfully
      submit : function(form, result){
      console.log('success', Ext.toArray(arguments));
    },
    //listener if the form submission fails
    exception : function(form, result){
      console.log('failure', Ext.toArray(arguments));
    }
  },

  //items docked to the bottom of the form
  dockedItems: [
    {
      xtype: 'toolbar',
      dock: 'bottom',
      items: [
        {
          text: 'Reset',
          handler: function() {
            form.reset();  //reset the fields
```

```
            }
          },
          {
            text: 'Save',
            ui: 'confirm',
            handler: function() {
              //submit the form data to the url
              form.submit();
            }
          }
                    ]
                }
        ]
      };

      if (Ext.is.Phone) {
        formBase.fullscreen = true;
      } else { //if desktop
          Ext.apply(formBase, {
              autoRender: true,
              floating: true,
              modal: true,
              centered: true,
              hideOnMaskTap: false,
              height: 385,
              width: 480
          });
      }
      //create form panel
      form = new Ext.form.FormPanel(formBase);
      form.show();  //render the form to the body
  }
});
```

3. Include the following line in `index.html`:

```
<script type="text/javascript" charset="utf-8"
  src="ch02/ch02_01.js"></script>
```

4. Deploy and access it from the browser. You will see the following screen:

How it works...

The code creates a form panel, with a field set inside it. The field set has four fields specified as part of its child items. `xtype` mentioned for each field instructs the Sencha Touch component manager which class to use to instantiate them.

`form = new Ext.form.FormPanel(formBase)` creates the form and the other field components using the config defined as part of the `formBase`.

`form.show()` renders the form to the body and that is how it will appear on the screen.

`url` contains the URL where the form data will be posted upon submission. The form can be submitted in the following
two ways:

1. By hitting **Go**, on the virtual keyboard or *Enter* on a field that ends up generating the action event.

2. By clicking on the **Save** button, which internally calls the `submit()` method on the form object.

`form.reset()` resets the status of the form and its fields to the original state. Therefore, if you had entered the values in the fields and clicked on the **Reset** button, all the fields would be cleared.

`form.submit()` posts the form data to the specified `url`. The data is posted as an Ajax request using the `POST` method.

Use of `useClearIcon` on the field instructs Sencha Touch whether it should show the clear icon in the field when the user starts entering a value in it. On clicking on this icon, the value in the field is cleared.

There's more...

In the preceding code, we saw how to construct a form panel, add fields to it, and handle events. We will see what other non-trivial things we may have to do in the project and how we can achieve these using Sencha Touch.

Standard submit

This is the old and traditional way for form data posting to the server `url`. If your application need is to use the standard form submit, rather than Ajax, then you will have to set `standardSubmit` to `true` on the form panel. This is set to `false`, by default. The following code snippet shows the usage of this property:

```
var formBase = {
    scroll: 'vertical',
    standardSubmit: true,
...
```

After this property is set to `true` on the `FormPanel`, `form.submit()` will load the complete page specified in `url`.

Do not submit on field action

As we saw earlier, the form data is automatically posted to the `url` if the action event (when the Go or *Enter* key is hit) occurs. In many applications, this default feature may not be desirable. In order to disable this feature, you will have to set `submitOnAction` to `false` on the form panel.

Post-submission handling

Say we posted our data to the `url`. Now, either the call may fail or it may succeed. In order to handle these specific conditions and act accordingly, we will have to pass additional config options to the form's `submit()` method. The following code shows the enhanced version of the `submit` call:

```
form.submit({
        success: function(form, result) {
            Ext.Msg.alert("INFO", "Form submitted!");
        },
        failure: function(form, result) {
            Ext.Msg.alert("INFO", "Form submission failed!");
        }
});
```

If the Ajax call (to post form data) fails, then the `failure` callback function is called, and in the case of success, the `success` callback function is called. This works only if the `standardSubmit` is set to `false`.

See also

- ▸ The recipe named *Setting up the Android-based development environment* in *Chapter 1*
- ▸ The recipe named *Setting up the iOS-based development environment* in *Chapter 1*
- ▸ The recipe named *Setting up the Blackberry-based development environment* in *Chapter 1*
- ▸ The recipe named *Setting up the browser-based development environment* in *Chapter 1*
- ▸ The recipe named *Setting up the production environment* in *Chapter 1*

Working with search

In this and the subsequent recipes of the chapter, we will go over each of the form fields and understand how to work with them. This recipe describes the steps required to create and use a search form field.

Getting ready

Make sure that you have set up your development environment by following the recipes outlined in *Chapter 1*.

Make sure that you have followed the *Getting your form ready with FormPanel* recipe.

How to do it...

Carry out the following steps:

1. Copy `ch02_01.js` to `ch02_02.js`.
2. Open a new file named `ch02_02.js` and replace the definition of `formBase` with the following code:

```
var formBase = {
  items: [{
    xtype: 'searchfield',
    name: 'search',
    label: 'Search'
  }]
};
```

3. Include `ch02_02.js` in place of `ch02_01.js` in `index.html`.

4. Deploy and access the application in the browser. You will see a form panel with a search field.

How it works...

The search field can be constructed by using the `Ext.form.Search` class instance or by using the `xtype—searchfield`. The search form field implements HTML5 `<input>` with `type="search"`. However, the implementation is very limited. For example, the HTML5 search field allows us to associate a data list to it which it can use during the search, whereas this feature is not present in Sencha Touch. Similarly, the W3 search field spec defines a `pattern` attribute to allow us to specify a regular expression against which a User Agent is meant to check the value, which is not supported yet in Sencha Touch. For more detail, you may refer to the W3 search field (`http://www.w3.org/TR/html-markup/input.search.html`) and the source code of the `Ext.form.Search` class.

There's more...

Often, in the application, for the search fields we do not use a label. Rather, we would like to show a text, such as **Search** inside the field that will disappear when the focus is on the field. Let's see how we can achieve this.

Using a placeholder

Placeholders are supported by most of the form fields in Sencha Touch by using the property `placeHolder`. The placeholder text appears in the field as long as there is no value entered in it and the field does not have the focus. The following code snippet shows the typical usage of it:

```
{
    xtype: 'searchfield',
    name: 'search',
    label: 'Search',
    placeHolder: 'Search...'
}
```

See also

▶ The recipe named *Setting up the Android-based development environment* in *Chapter 1*

▶ The recipe named *Setting up the iOS-based development environment* in *Chapter 1*

▶ The recipe named *Setting up the Blackberry-based development environment* in *Chapter 1*

> ▶ The recipe named *Setting up the browser-based development environment* in *Chapter 1*

> ▶ The recipe named *Setting up the production environment* in *Chapter 1*

> ▶ The recipe named *Getting your form ready with FormPanel* in this chapter

Putting custom validation in the e-mail field

This recipe describes how to make use of the e-mail form field provided by Sencha Touch and how to validate the value entered into it to find out whether the entered e-mail passes the validation rule or not.

Getting ready

Make sure that you have set up your development environment by following the recipes outlined in *Chapter 1*.

Make sure that you have followed the *Getting your form ready with FormPanel* recipe in this chapter.

How to do it...

Carry out the following steps:

1. Copy `ch02_01.js` to `ch02_03.js`.

2. Open a new file named `ch02_03.js` and replace the definition of `formBase` with the following code:

```
var formBase = {
  items: [{
    xtype: 'emailfield',
    name : 'email',
    label: 'Email',
    placeHolder: 'you@sencha.com',
    useClearIcon: true,
    listeners: {
      blur: function(thisTxt, eventObj) {
        var val = thisTxt.getValue();

        //validate using the pattern
        if (val.search("[a-c]+@[a-z]+[.][a-z]+") == -1)
          Ext.Msg.alert("Error", "Invalid e-mail address!!");
        else
          Ext.Msg.alert("Info", "Valid e-mail address!!");
```

```
            }
         }
      }]
   };
```

3. Include `ch02_03.js` in place of `ch02_02.js` in `index.html`.

4. Deploy and access the application in the browser.

How it works...

The e-mail field can be constructed by using the `Ext.form.Email` class instance or by using the `xtype: emailfield`. The e-mail form field implements HTML5 `<input>` with `type="email."` However, as with the search field, the implementation is very limited. For example, the HTML5 e-mail field allows us to specify a regular expression pattern which can be used to validate the value entered in the field.

See also

▶ The recipe named *Setting up the Android-based development environment* in *Chapter 1*

▶ The recipe named *Setting up the iOS-based development environment* in *Chapter 1*

▶ The recipe named *Setting up the Blackberry-based development environment* in *Chapter 1*

▶ The recipe named *Setting up the browser-based development environment* in *Chapter 1*

▶ The recipe named *Setting up the production environment* in *Chapter 1*

▶ The recipe named *Getting your form ready with FormPanel* in this chapter

Working with dates using DatePicker

This recipe describes how to make use of the date picker form field provided by Sencha Touch, which allows the user to select a date.

Getting ready

Make sure that you have set up your development environment by following the recipes outlined in *Chapter 1*.

Make sure that you have followed the *Getting your form ready with FormPanel* recipe in this chapter.

Carry out the following steps:

1. Copy ch02_01.js to ch02_04.js.

2. Open a new file named ch02_04.js and replace the definition of formBase with the following code:

```
var formBase = {
  items: [{
    xtype: 'datepickerfield',
    name: 'date',
    label: 'Date'
  }]
};
```

3. Include ch02_04.js in place of ch02_03.js in index.html.

4. Deploy and access the application in the browser.

The date picker field can be constructed by using the Ext.form.DatePicker class instance or by using xtype: datepickerfield. The date picker form field implements HTML <select>. When the user tries to select an entry, it shows the date picker with the month, day, and year slots for selection. After selection, when the user clicks on the **Done** button, the field is set with the selected value.

Additionally, there are other things that can be done such as setting the date to the current date, or any particular date, or changing the order of appearance of a month, day, and year. Let's see what it takes to accomplish this.

Setting the default date to the current date

In order to set the default value to the current date, the value property must be set to the current date. The following code shows how to do it:

```
var formBase = {
  items: [{
    xtype: 'datepickerfield',
    name: 'date',
    label: 'Date',
    value: new Date(),
```

Setting the default date to a particular date

The default date is 01/01/1970. Let's assume that you need to set the date to a different date, but not the current date. To do so, you will have to set the `value` using the `year`, `month`, and `day` properties, as follows:

```
var formBase = {
  items: [{
    xtype: 'datepickerfield',
    name: 'date',
    label: 'Date',
    value: {year: 2011, month: 6, day: 11},
...
```

Changing the slot order

By default, the slot order is month, day, and year. You can change it by setting the `slotOrder` property of the `picker` property of date picker, as shown in the following code:

```
var formBase = {
  items: [{
    xtype: 'datepickerfield',
    name: 'date',
    label: 'Date',
    picker: {slotOrder: ['day', 'month', 'year']}
  }]
};
```

Setting the picker date range

By default, the date range shown by the picker is 1970 until the current year. For our application need, if we have to alter the year range, we can do so by setting the `yearFrom` and `yearTo` properties of the `picker` property of the date picker, as follows:

```
var formBase = {
  items: [{
    xtype: 'datepickerfield',
    name: 'date',
    label: 'Date',
    picker: {yearFrom: 2000, yearTo: 2010}
  }]
};
```

See also

▸ The recipe named *Setting up the Android-based development environment* in *Chapter 1*

▸ The recipe named *Setting up the iOS-based development environment* in *Chapter 1*

▸ The recipe named *Setting up the Blackberry-based development environment* in *Chapter 1*

▸ The recipe named *Setting up the browser-based development environment* in *Chapter 1*

▸ The recipe named *Setting up the production environment* in *Chapter 1*

▸ The recipe named *Getting your form ready with FormPanel* in this chapter

Making a field hidden

Often in an application, there would be a need to hide fields which are not needed in a particular context but are required and hence need to be shown in another. In this recipe, we will see how to make a field hidden and show it, conditionally.

Getting ready

Make sure that you have set up your development environment by following the recipes outlined in *Chapter 1*.

Make sure that you have followed the *Getting your form ready with FormPanel* recipe in this chapter.

How to do it...

Carry out the following steps:

1. Edit `ch02_04.js` and modify the code as follows by adding the `hidden` property:

```
var formBase = {
  items: [{
    xtype: 'datepickerfield',
    id: 'datefield-id',
    name: 'date',
    hidden: true,
    label: 'Date'}]
};
```

2. Deploy and access the application in the browser.

How it works...

When a field is marked as hidden, Sencha Touch uses the DOM's `hide` method on the element to hide that particular field.

There's more...

Let's see how we can programmatically show/hide a field.

Showing/Hiding a field at runtime

Each component in Sencha Touch supports two methods: `show` and `hide`. The `show` method shows the element and `hide` hides the element. In order to call these methods, we will have to first find the reference to the component, which can be achieved by either using the object reference or by using the `Ext.getCmp()` method. Given a component ID, the `getCmp` method returns us the component. The following code snippet demonstrates how to show an element:

```
var cmp = Ext.getCmp('datefield-id');
cmp.show();
```

To hide an element, we will have to call `cmp.hide();`

See also

- ▶ The recipe named *Setting up the Android-based development environment* in *Chapter 1*
- ▶ The recipe named *Setting up the iOS-based development environment* in *Chapter 1*
- ▶ The recipe named *Setting up the Blackberry-based development environment* in *Chapter 1*
- ▶ The recipe named *Setting up the browser-based development environment* in *Chapter 1*
- ▶ The recipe named *Setting up the production environment* in *Chapter 1*
- ▶ The recipe named *Getting your form ready with FormPanel* in this chapter

Working with the select field

This recipe describes the use of the select form field, which allows the user to select a value from a list of choices, such as a combo box.

Getting ready

Make sure that you have set up your development environment by following the recipes outlined in *Chapter 1*.

Make sure that you have followed the *Getting your form ready with FormPanel* recipe in this chapter.

How to do it...

Carry out the following steps:

1. Copy `ch02_01.js` to `ch02_05.js`.

2. Open a new file named `ch02_05.js` and replace the definition of `formBase` with the following code:

```
var formBase = {
    items: [{
            xtype: 'selectfield',
            name: 'select',
            label: 'Select',
            placeHolder: 'Select...',
        options: [
            {text: 'First Option',  value: 'first'},
            {text: 'Second Option', value: 'second'},
            {text: 'Third Option',  value: 'third'}
        ]
        }]
};
```

3. Include `ch02_05.js` in place of `ch02_04.js` in `index.html`.

4. Deploy and access the application in the browser.

How it works...

The preceding code creates a select form field with the three options for selection. The select field can be constructed by using the `Ext.form.Select` class instance or by using the `xtype—selectfield`. The select form field implements HTML `<select>`. By default, it uses the `text` property to show the text for selection.

There's more...

It may not always be possible or desirable to use `text` and `value` properties in the date to populate the selection list. If we have a different property in place of `text`, then how do we make sure that the selection list is populated correctly without any further conversion? Let's see how we can do this.

Using the custom display value

We, use `displayField` to specify the field that will be used as text, as shown in the following code:

```
{
  xtype: 'selectfield',
  name: 'select',
  label: 'Second Select',
  placeHolder: 'Select...',
  displayField: 'desc',
  hiddenName: 'second-select'
  ,options: [
    {desc: 'First Option',  value: 'first'},
    {desc: 'Second Option', value: 'second'},
    {desc: 'Third Option',  value: 'third'}
  ]
}
```

See also

▶ The recipe named *Setting up the Android-based development environment* in *Chapter 1*

▶ The recipe named *Setting up the iOS-based development environment* in *Chapter 1*

▶ The recipe named *Setting up the Blackberry-based development environment* in *Chapter 1*

▶ The recipe named *Setting up the browser-based development environment* in *Chapter 1*

▶ The recipe named *Setting up the production environment* in *Chapter 1*

▶ The recipe named *Getting your form ready with FormPanel* in this chapter

Changing the value using Slider

This recipe describes the use of the Slider form field, which allows the user to change the value by merely sliding.

Getting ready

Make sure that you have set up your development environment by following the recipes outlined in *Chapter 1*.

Make sure that you have followed the *Get your form ready with FormPanel* recipe in this chapter.

How to do it...

Carry out the following steps:

1. Copy `ch02_01.js` to `ch02_06.js`.
2. Open a new file named `ch02_06.js` and replace the definition of `formBase` with the following code:

```
var formBase = {
  items: [{
    xtype: 'sliderfield',
    name : 'height',
    label: 'Height',
    minValue: 0,
    maxValue: 100,
    increment: 10
  }]
};
```

3. Include `ch02_06.js` in place of `ch02_05.js` in `index.html`.
4. Deploy and access the application in the browser.

How it works...

The preceding code creates a slider field with 0–100 as the range of values, with 10 as the `increment`, which means when a user clicks on the slider, the value will change by 10 on every click. The `increment` value must be a whole number.

See also

- The recipe named *Setting up the Android-based development environment* in *Chapter 1*
- The recipe named *Setting up the iOS-based development environment* in *Chapter 1*
- The recipe named *Setting up the Blackberry-based development environment* in *Chapter 1*
- The recipe named *Setting up the browser-based development environment* in *Chapter 1*
- The recipe named *Setting up the production environment* in *Chapter 1*
- The recipe named *Getting your form ready with FormPanel* in this chapter

Spinning the number wheel using Spinner

This recipe describes the use of a spinner form field, which allows the user to change the value by clicking on the wheel.

Getting ready

Make sure that you have set up your development environment by following the recipes outlined in *Chapter 1*.

Make sure that you have followed the *Getting your form ready with FormPanel* recipe in this chapter.

How to do it...

Carry out the following steps:

1. Copy `ch02_01.js` to `ch02_07.js`.
2. Open a new file named `ch02_07.js` and replace the definition of `formBase` with the following code:

```
var formBase = {
  items: [{
    xtype: 'spinnerfield',
    name : 'spinner',
    label: 'Spinner',
    minValue: 0,
    maxValue: 100,
    incrementValue: 10,
    cycle: true
  }]
};
```

3. Include `ch02_07.js` in place of `ch02_06.js` in `index.html`.

4. Deploy and access the application in the browser.

How it works...

Spinner is a wrapper around the HTML5 number field. A spinner field can be constructed by using the `Ext.form.Spinner` class instance or by using the `xtype—spinnerfield`. `minValue` sets the initial value which will be displayed in the field when the field is rendered. `maxValue: 100` is the maximum value that will be displayed in this field. `incrementValue` instructs the framework that on every click the value will be incremented/decremented by 10, based on the direction in which the user is moving.

There's more...

In the spinner, it may be a more sensible thing to recycle the value. The following section shows how to do this.

Recycling the values

By default, when the user reaches the `maxValue` or the `minValue`, he/she cannot move further. In this case, we may want to recycle the values. In order to do this, the `spinner` class provides a `cycle` property and setting its value to `true` will ensure that the value is set to `minValue` when the user clicks after the field value had reached the `maxValue` and vice versa. The following code snippet shows how to set this property:

```
items: [{
  xtype: 'spinnerfield',
  name : 'spinner',
  label: 'Spinner',
  minValue: 0,
  maxValue: 100,
  incrementValue: 10,
  cycle: true
}]
```

See also

▶ The recipe named *Setting up the Android-based development environment* in *Chapter 1*

▶ The recipe named *Setting up the iOS-based development environment* in *Chapter 1*

▶ The recipe named *Setting up the Blackberry-based development environment* in *Chapter 1*

- ▶ The recipe named *Setting up the browser-based development environment* in *Chapter 1*
- ▶ The recipe named *Setting up the production environment* in *Chapter 1*
- ▶ The recipe named *Getting your form ready with FormPanel* in this chapter

Toggling between your two choices

This is a specialized slider with only two values. In this recipe, we will see how to make use of the `toggle` field.

Getting ready

Make sure that you have set up your development environment by following the recipes outlined in *Chapter 1*.

Make sure that you have followed the *Getting your form ready with FormPanel* recipe. in this chapter

How to do it...

Carry out the following steps:

1. Copy `ch02_01.js` to `ch02_08.js`.
2. Open a new file named `ch02_08.js` and replace the definition of `formBase` with the following code:

```
var formBase = {
  items: [{
    xtype: 'togglefield',
    name : 'toggle',
    label: 'Toggle'
  }]
};
```

3. Include `ch02_08.js` in place of `ch02_07.js` in `index.html`.
4. Deploy and access the application in the browser.

How it works...

This creates a `slider` field with the `minValue` set to `0` and `maxValue` set to `1`.

See also

- ▸ The recipe named *Setting up the Android-based development environment* in *Chapter 1*
- ▸ The recipe named *Setting up the iOS-based development environment* in *Chapter 1*
- ▸ The recipe named *Setting up the Blackberry-based development environment* in *Chapter 1*
- ▸ The recipe named *Setting up the browser-based development environment* in *Chapter 1*
- ▸ The recipe named *Setting up the production environment* in *Chapter 1*
- ▸ The recipe named *Getting your form ready with FormPanel* in this chapter

Checkbox and Checkbox group

Checkboxes permit the user to make multiple selections from a number of available options. It is a convenient way to learn about user choices. For example, in an application, we may have a checkbox asking the user if he/she stayed in Hyderabad. Moreover, if we are capturing the detail about multiple cities where the user had stayed, then we would group multiple checkboxes under one name and use them as a checkbox group. In this recipe, we will see how we can create a checkbox and a checkbox group using Sencha Touch and how to handle the values when you want to set them, or when the form data is posted.

Getting ready

Make sure that you have set up your development environment by following the recipes outlined in *Chapter 1*.

Make sure that you have followed the *Getting your form ready with FormPanel* recipe in this chapter.

How to do it...

Carry out the following steps:

1. Copy `ch02_01.js` to `ch02_09.js`.
2. Open a new file named `ch02_09.js` and replace the definition of `formBase` with the following code:

```
var formBase = {
  items: [{
    xtype: 'checkboxfield',
    name: 'city',
    value: 'Hyderabad',
```

```
        label: 'Hyderabad',
        checked: true
        }, {
          xtype: 'checkboxfield',
          name: 'city',
          value: 'Mumbai',
          label: 'Mumbai'
    }]
};
```

3. Include `ch02_09.js` in place of `ch02_08.js` in `index.html`.

4. Deploy and access the application in the browser. You will see the checkboxes as shown in the following screenshot:

How it works...

The preceding code creates two checkboxes inside the form panel. `checked: true` checks the checkbox when it is rendered. When a form is submitted, the checkbox values are returned as an array. For example, given the preceding code, when the user clicks on **Submit**, city would have two values, as follows:

```
city: ['Hyderabad', 'Mumbai']
```

See also

▸ The recipe named *Setting up the Android-based development environment* in *Chapter 1*

▸ The recipe named *Setting up the iOS-based development environment* in *Chapter 1*

▸ The recipe named *Setting up the Blackberry-based development environment* in *Chapter 1*

▸ The recipe named *Setting up the browser-based development environment* in *Chapter 1*

▸ The recipe named *Setting up the production environment* in *Chapter 1*

▸ The recipe named *Getting your form ready with FormPanel* in this chapter

Text and TextArea

Text fields are one of the initial fields which allow the user to enter data in a form. Text area allows entering multiple lines of text. In this recipe, we will make use of the text and text area related classes.

Getting ready

Make sure that you have set up your development environment by following the recipes outlined in *Chapter 1*.

Make sure that you have followed the *Getting your form ready with FormPanel* recipe in this chapter.

How to do it...

Carry out the following steps:

1. Copy `ch02_01.js` to `ch02_10.js`.

2. Open a new file named `ch02_10.js` and replace the definition of `formBase` with the following code:

```
var formBase = {
  items: [
    {
      xtype: 'textfield',
      name : 'firstName',
      label: 'First Name'
    },
    {
      xtype: 'textfield',
```

```
          name : 'lastName',
          label: 'Last Name'
        },
        {
          xtype: 'textareafield',
          name : 'detail',
          label: 'Detail'
        }
      ]
    };
```

3. Include `ch02_10.js` in place of `ch02_09.js` in `index.html`.

4. Deploy and access the application in the browser.

How it works...

In the preceding code, we created two text fields and a text area. Text field can be constructed by using the `Ext.form.Text` class instance or by using the `xtype—textfield`. Similarly, a text area can be constructed by using the `Ext.form.TextArea` class instance or by using `xtype—textareafield`. Internally, the text form field implements the HTML `<input>` element with `type="text"` whereas text area implements the HTML `<textarea>` element. There is no validation on these fields, hence the user is allowed, by default, to enter any kind of value.

There's more...

By default, a text field or a text area allows entering any number of characters. However, in some specific scenarios, we may have to limit this to a particular value in our application. Let's see how we can limit this.

Limiting the number of input characters

Both text field and text area support a property named `maxLength` which controls the number of characters the user can enter. If this property is set to 20, then the user can only enter 20 characters. The following code snippet shows how to do this:

```
{
  xtype: 'textfield',
  name : 'firstName',
  maxLength: 20,
  label: 'First Name'
},
{
  xtype: 'textareafield',
  name : 'detail',
  maxLength: 80,
```

```
        label: 'Detail'
    }
```

See also

▸ The recipe named *Setting up the Android-based development environment* in *Chapter 1*

▸ The recipe named *Setting up the iOS-based development environment* in *Chapter 1*

▸ The recipe named *Setting up the Blackberry-based development environment* in *Chapter 1*

▸ The recipe named *Setting up the browser-based development environment* in *Chapter 1*

▸ The recipe named *Setting up the production environment* in *Chapter 1*

▸ The recipe named *Getting your form ready with FormPanel* in this chapter

Grouping fields with FieldSet

FieldSet is used to logically group together elements in a form, an example of which we saw in the first recipe of this chapter. This recipe shows how the Sencha Touch class can be used to create and group items under FieldSet.

Getting ready

Make sure that you have set up your development environment by following the recipes outlined in *Chapter 1*.

Make sure that you have followed the *Getting your form ready with FormPanel* recipe in this chapter.

How to do it...

Carry out the following steps:

1. Copy `ch02_01.js` to `ch02_12.js`.

2. Open a new file named `ch02_12.js` and replace the definition of `formBase` with the following code:

```
var formBase = {
  items: [
    {
       xtype: 'fieldset',
       title: 'About Me',
       items: [
```

```
          {
            xtype: 'textfield',
            name : 'firstName',
            label: 'First Name'
          },
          {
            xtype: 'textfield',
            name : 'lastName',
            label: 'Last Name'
          }
        ]
      }
    ]
  };
```

3. Include ch02_12.js in place of ch02_10.js in index.html.
4. Deploy and access the application in the browser.

How it works...

FieldSets can be constructed by using the Ext.form.FieldSet class instance or by using the xtype—fieldset. All elements which must be grouped under the field set must be added to the field set as child items. The FieldSet class implements the HTML <fieldset> element and uses legend to show the title.

There's more...

Suppose, when you are grouping the elements under the field set, you also want a way to add some instructions for it, to give more information to the user. The FieldSet class supports this and we will now see how to do it.

Adding instructions

The Ext.form.FieldSet class provides a property named instructions which we can use to add additional instructions. The following code snippet shows how to set this property:

```
xtype: 'fieldset',
title: 'About Me',
instructions: 'Fill in your personal detail',
...
```

The specified instruction is added at the bottom of the field set as shown in the following screenshot:

See also

- ▶ The recipe named *Setting up the Android-based development environment* in *Chapter 1*
- ▶ The recipe named *Setting up the iOS-based development environment* in *Chapter 1*
- ▶ The recipe named *Setting up the Blackberry-based development environment* in *Chapter 1*
- ▶ The recipe named *Setting up the browser-based development environment* in *Chapter 1*
- ▶ The recipe named *Setting up the production environment* in *Chapter 1*
- ▶ The recipe named *Getting your form ready with FormPanel* in this chapter

Validating your form

So far, we have looked at how to create a form and make use of different form fields offered by Sencha Touch. Different form fields provide different kinds of information a user can enter. Now, some of them may be valid and some may not. It is a common practice to validate the form and the entered values at the time of posting. Now, based on your application architecture, you may choose to apply all kinds of validations in the frontend UI, or you may choose to handle them in the backend server code, or a combination of the two. All are valid approaches. However, for this chapter, we would assume that we want to validate the form on the frontend to make sure that the values entered are valid.

Sencha Touch does not offer a mechanism to do form validation. As of now, it has no direct support for validating the inputs. If we intend to validate the form, then the code has to be written to do so. There are various approaches to building the form validation capability, depending upon what level of abstraction and re-usability we want to achieve. We can write a specific code in each form to carry out the validation or we can enhance `Ext.Component`, which is the base class for all the Sencha Touch components, or the `Ext.form.Field` classes to handle the validation in a more generic way. Alternatively, we can enhance `FormPanel`, as well, to implement a nicely encapsulated form and field validation functionality. In this recipe, we will see how we can write the specific validation code to take care of our need. The author hopes that there will be a more streamlined validation in a future version of Sencha Touch.

Getting ready

Make sure that you have set up your development environment by following the recipes outlined in *Chapter 1*.

Make sure that you have followed the *Getting your form ready with FormPanel* recipe in this chapter.

How to do it...

Carry out the following steps:

1. Copy `ch02_01.js` to `ch02_13.js` and modify the `handler` function with the following code:

```
handler: function() {
  var isValid = true;
  var errors = new Array();

  var fieldValMap = form.getValues();
  var email = fieldValMap['email'];
  var name = fieldValMap['name'];
```

```
        //validate the name
        if (name.search(/[0-9]/) > -1) {
          isValid = false;
          errors.push({field : 'name',
          reason : 'Name must not contain numbers'});
        }

        //validate e-mail
        if (email.search("@") == -1) {
          isValid = false;
          errors.push({field : 'email',
          reason : 'E-mail address must contain @'});
        }

        //show error if the validation failed
        if (!isValid) {
          var errStr = "";

          Ext.each(errors, function(error, index){
            errStr += "[" + (index+1) + "] - " + error.reason + "\n";
          });

          Ext.Msg.alert("Error", errStr);
        } else {//form is valid
          form.submit();
        }
      }
```

2. Include ch02_13.js in place of ch02_12.js in index.html.

3. Deploy and access the application in the browser.

How it works...

The handler function is called when the user clicks on the **Save** button. The handler validates the name and the e-mail address field values. name.search(/[0-9]/) checks if the name entered contains any numbers and email.search("@") verifies if the e-mail address contains @ or not. In case of an error, we are adding an error object to the errors array with two properties: field and reason. The field property stores the field on which the validation had failed and the corresponding reason is stored in the reason property. After all the fields have been validated, we are checking the isValid flag to see if any of the field validation had failed and, if so, we show up a message box with the list of errors, as shown in the following screenshot:

If there are no field validation errors, then the form is submitted.

See also

> ▸ The recipe named *Setting up the Android-based development environment* in *Chapter 1*

> ▸ The recipe named *Setting up the iOS-based development environment* in *Chapter 1*

> ▸ The recipe named *Setting up the Blackberry-based development environment* in *Chapter 1*

> ▸ The recipe named *Setting up the browser-based development environment* in *Chapter 1*

> ▸ The recipe named *Setting up the production environment* in *Chapter 1*

> ▸ The recipe named *Getting your form ready with FormPanel* in this chapter

3
Containers and Layouts

In this chapter, we will cover:

- ► Keeping the container lightweight
- ► Working with Panel
- ► Adding items to a container at runtime
- ► Building wizards using CardLayout
- ► Panel docking using DockLayout
- ► Fitting into the container using FitLayout
- ► Arranging items horizontally using HBoxLayout
- ► Arranging items vertically using VBoxLayout
- ► Mixing layouts

Introduction

Containers in Sencha Touch are components which can contain other components. They handle the basic behavior of containing items, namely adding and removing items. In the previous chapter, we talked about the form and the different form fields. A form is a container. Other containers are `Panel`, `TabPanel`, `Sheet`, `NestedList`, `Carousel`, `FieldSet`, `Toolbar`, and so on. All the container classes extend the `Ext.Container` class.

The following diagram depicts the various container classes and their relationship with each other:

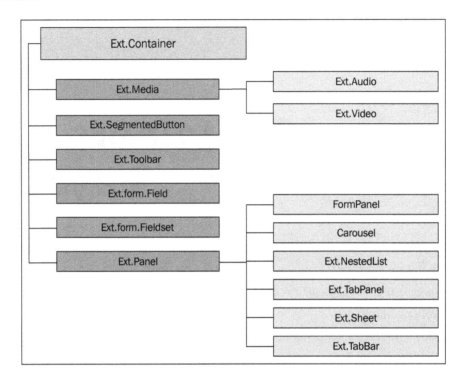

Ext.Container is the base class, which provides the basic common functionalities related to a container and it is extended further by the different classes which implement certain specific behaviors. For example, Toolbar takes care of showing various buttons in the form of a toolbar whereas Media takes care of playing the audio/video.

In order to implement a new container, you may extend one of the existing specific container classes, such as TabPanel extending Panel, which is very close to your requirement. In the worst case, you will have to extend the Ext.Container class.

When we go on adding items (fields, panel, etc.) to a container, an obvious question is how will these items be rendered and positioned on the page? Will they be rendered one after another, vertically? Will they be rendered horizontally? Will they be resized when we resize the page? The answer to all these questions is **layout**. A layout takes care of the sizing, re-sizing, and positioning of the children of a container. Every container in Sencha Touch has a config property named `layout`, which accepts the name of the layout that needs to be used to calculate the sizing and position of the children. The following are the pre-defined values and how they layout the child items:

Layout	Description
auto	Renders one item after another
card	Renders each item as a card and only one item is visible at any given time
dock	Handles docking for panels
fit	Renders a single item and automatically expands to fill the layout's container
hbox	Arranges items horizontally across a container
vbox	Arranges items vertically down a container

The following diagram depicts the different layout related classes and the way they are related to each other:

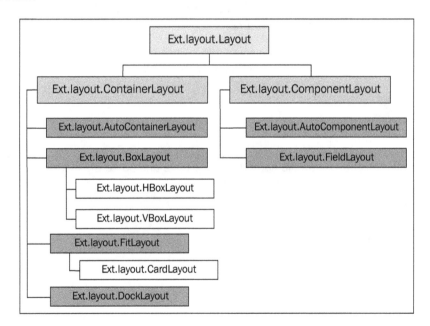

Ext.Panel is the default container class and auto is the default container layout used by Sencha Touch.

Some of the containers we have already used in the previous chapter and we will use the other ones in this and the subsequent chapters. In this chapter, we will look into different containers and the use of layouts to position the items.

Keeping the container lightweight

We saw earlier in this chapter that Ext.Container is the base class for all the containers. It gives the basic building block and the specific behaviors are implemented in the respective specific containers. Ext.Panel acts as a generic container class with the support for docking. If your application only needs a container so that you can add items to it and they are rendered, then you should go for Ext.Container rather than using Ext.Panel. In this recipe, we will see how to make use of Ext.Container to contain our item.

Getting ready

Make sure that you have set up your development environment by following the recipes outlined in *Chapter 1, Gear up for the Journey*.

Create a new folder named ch03 in the same folder where we created the ch01 and ch02 folders. We will be using this new folder for keeping the code.

How to do it...

Carry out the following steps:

1. Create and open a new file named ch03_01.js and paste the following code into it:

```
Ext.setup({
  onReady: function() {

    var pnl = new Ext.Container({
      fullscreen: true,
      defaults: {
        border: false
      },
      items: [{
          bodyStyle: 'background:grey;',
          html: '<p>Panel 1</p>'
        },{
          xtype: 'textfield',
```

```
          name : 'first',
          label: 'First name'
        },
        {
          xtype: 'textfield',
          name : 'last',
          label: 'Last name'
        },
        {
          xtype: 'numberfield',
          name : 'age',
          label: 'Age'
        },
        {
          xtype: 'urlfield',
          name : 'url',
          label: 'Website'
      }]
    });
      }
  });
```

2. Update the index.html file.

3. Deploy and access it from the browser. You will see the panel with items as shown in the following screenshot:

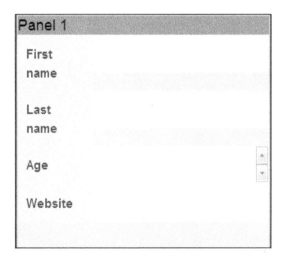

How it works...

The preceding code creates a container with a panel and four form fields. The following is the first child item being added to the container:

```
{
    bodyStyle: 'background:grey;',
    html: '<p>Panel 1</p>'
}
```

As there is no `xtype` specified, Sencha Touch creates `Ext.Panel` and sets the `bodyStyle` and `html` on it.

The default layout used is `auto`; hence, we see the items are rendered one after another.

There's more...

While we are using `Ext.Container` for its lightweight nature, we may need our items to be laid out differently. Let's see how we can do this.

Using layout

The `Ext.Container` class supports the `layout` property, which we can set to request the container to position and calculate sizing accordingly. The following are the layouts that can be used with `Ext.Container`:

- auto
- fit
- card
- hbox
- vbox

For example adding the following additional properties on `Ext.Container` would show the first panel in the whole screen:

```
layout: 'card',
activeItem: 0
```

See also

- ▸ The recipe named *Setting up the browser-based development environment* in *Chapter 1*
- ▸ The recipe named *Getting your form ready with FormPanel* in *Chapter 2*
- ▸ The recipe named *Panel docking using DockLayout* in this chapter

Working with Panel

Ext.Panel is a specific implementation of a generic container by extending the Ext. Container. The main functionality that it provides on top of the Ext.Container is the support for docking items. We can add any number of items to it, which it can dock. This recipe describes how to make use of the Ext.Panel class to create an application.

Getting ready

Make sure that you have set up your development environment by following the recipes outlined in *Chapter 1*.

How to do it...

Carry out the following steps:

1. Create and open a new file named ch03_02.js and paste the following code into it:

```
Ext.setup({
    onReady: function() {

    var pnl = new Ext.Panel({
        fullscreen: true,
        defaults: {
            border: false
        },
        items: [{
            bodyStyle: 'background:grey;',
            html: '<p>Panel 1</p>'
          },{
                xtype: 'textfield',
                name : 'first',
                label: 'First name'
            },
            {
```

```
                         xtype: 'textfield',
                         name : 'last',
                         label: 'Last name'
                    },
                    {

                         xtype: 'numberfield',
                         name : 'age',
                         label: 'Age'
                    },
                    {

                         xtype: 'urlfield',
                         name : 'url',
                         label: 'Website'
                }]
            });
            }
        });
```

2. Update the `index.html` file.
3. Deploy and access it from the browser.

How it works...

The preceding code creates a panel with a panel and four form fields. The default layout used is `auto`.

There's more...

Additionally, we can use a different layout and also have the docking items with a panel. Let's see how we can make use of these features.

Docking items

As we discussed earlier, one of the major advantages of using `Ext.Panel` over `Ext.Container` is that it can dock one or more items. This is driven by the config—`dockedItems`. It accepts the items that can be specified as part of the `items` config. This config property instructs `Ext.Panel` that these items need to be docked and it uses the `dock` layout to position them and calculate their sizing.

The following code shows that we are adding a toolbar with two buttons, **Save** and **Reset**, as the dock item:

```
dockedItems: [
    {
       xtype: 'toolbar',
```

```
      dock: 'bottom',
      items: [
        {
          text: 'Reset',
          handler: function() {

          }
        },
        {
          text: 'Save',
          ui: 'confirm',
          handler: function() {
            Ext.Msg.alert("INFO", "In real implementation, this
              will be saved!");
          }
        }
      ]
    }
  ]
```

`dock: 'bottom'` is a dock layout specific property which instructs that the toolbar needs to be positioned at the bottom of the panel. In the dock panel, we have added two buttons, **Reset** and **Save**. The following screenshot shows how the screen will look:

Using layouts

Similar to `Ext.Container`, `Ext.Panel` also supports the `layout` property, which can be used to set the appropriate layout. The following are the layouts that can be used with `Ext.Panel`:

- auto
- fit
- dock
- card
- hbox
- vbox

The `dock` layout is not specified explicitly. Rather, based on the `dockedItems` config property the container uses this layout internally.

See also

- The recipe named *Setting up the browser-based development environment* in *Chapter 1*
- The recipe named *Panel docking using DockLayout* in this chapter

Adding items to a container at runtime

In an application, there would be numerous scenarios where we would have to add components ranging from a simple field to a panel at runtime as part of the response to the user event. For example, your application may have a payment panel where you may want to show the payment specific detail panels based on the payment method. If a user selects `Credit Card` as the payment method, then you may show a panel asking the user to enter their credit card detail. This requires us to add components dynamically to an existing container. In this recipe, we will see how to work with components at runtime.

Getting ready

Make sure that you have set up your development environment by following the recipes outlined in *Chapter 1*.

How to do it...

Carry out the following steps:

1. Create and open a new file named `ch03_03.js` and paste the following code into it:

```
Ext.setup({
    onReady: function() {

        var pnl = new Ext.Panel({
            fullscreen: true,
            defaults: {
                border: false
            },
            items: [{
                    xtype: 'textfield',
                    name : 'first',
                    label: 'First name'
                },
                {
                    xtype: 'textfield',
                    name : 'last',
                    label: 'Last name'
                },
                {
                    xtype: 'numberfield',
                    name : 'age',
                    label: 'Age'
                },
                {
                    xtype: 'urlfield',
                    name : 'url',
                    label: 'Website'
            }],
            dockedItems: [
                {
                    xtype: 'toolbar',
                    dock: 'bottom',
                    items: [
                        {
                            text: 'Reset',
                            handler: function() {

                            }
                        },
```

```
              {
                text: 'Add',
                ui: 'confirm',
                handler: function() {
                  Ext.Msg.alert("INFO", "This will add a new
                    e-mail field to the panel!");
                  pnl.add({
                    xtype: 'emailfield',

                    name : 'email',
                    label: 'E-mail'
                  });
                  pnl.addDocked({
                    xtype : 'toolbar',
                    dock: 'top',
                    items: [{
                      text: 'Dummy'
                    }]
                  });
                  pnl.doLayout();
                }
              }
            ]
          }
        ]
      });

    }
  });
```

2. Update the `index.html` file.

3. Deploy and access it from the browser.

How it works...

The code creates a panel with three form fields and two buttons, **Add** and **Reset**. When the user clicks on the **Add** button, a new e-mail field is added to the panel and a new toolbar with a **Dummy** button is added to the docked items. The following code in the **Add** button handler adds an e-mail field and a docked item to the panel:

```
pnl.add({
  xtype: 'emailfield',
  name : 'email',
  label: 'E-mail'
```

```
});

pnl.addDocked({
    xtype : 'toolbar',
    dock: 'top',
    items: [{
      text: 'Dummy'
    }]
});
```

When the items are added to the panel, the panel does not automatically do the rendering and size calculation. The addDocked method internally calls the doComponentLayout and hence the toolbar is rendered with the button and we can see it. However, this does not happen in the case of the add method. Due to this, even though the e-mail field is added to the panel, we don't see it appearing on the screen. To ensure that the newly added component shows up after addition at runtime, the following line must be added where the doLayout method is called on the container:

```
pnl.doLayout();
```

The doLayout method invokes the layout manager associated with the container. In this case, as we have not specified layout property, the auto layout manager will be invoked which will add the **E-mail** field after the **Website**. The following screenshot shows how the screen will look before and after clicking on the **Add** button:

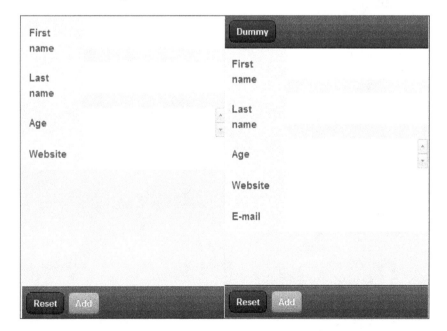

Additionally, we can use a different layout and also have the docking items with a panel. Let's see how we can make use of these features.

Inserting at a specific position

The `insert` and `insertDocked` methods allow us to insert a component at the desired position. For example, the following code will add the e-mail field before the **Website**:

```
pnl.insert(3, {
  xtype: 'emailfield',
  name : 'email',
  label: 'E-mail'
});
```

Removing an item

In order to remove an item, the container provides `remove` and `removeAll` methods to remove one or all components, respectively. In order to remove a particular component, we need either its ID or its object reference. In the following code snippet, we have added an ID, `email-id`, to the e-mail field that we are creating and when the user clicks on the **Reset** button, we are removing it from the panel:

```
dockedItems: [
  {
    xtype: 'toolbar',
    dock: 'bottom',
    items: [
      {
        text: 'Reset',
        handler: function() {
          //remove the added e-mail field
          pnl.remove('email-id');
        }
      },
      {
        text: 'Add',
        ui: 'confirm',
        handler: function() {
          Ext.Msg.alert("INFO", "This will add a new e-mail
            field to the panel!");
          pnl.add({
            xtype: 'emailfield',
            id: 'email-id',
            name : 'email',
```

```
            label: 'E-mail'
          });
          pnl.doLayout();
        }
      }
    ]
  }
]
```

Hiding/Showing

Sometimes in your application the user will be seeing a field based on some conditions. Moreover, if your application was doing this repeatedly, then add and remove may not be an efficient set of methods to use. Rather, we should use show and hide methods to control the visibility of a component. The following code snippet shows how a component can be hidden and shown again:

```
dockedItems: [
  {
    xtype: 'toolbar',
    dock: 'bottom',
    items: [
      {
        text: 'Reset',
        handler: function() {
          //hide the added e-mail field
          var cmp = Ext.getCmp('email-id');
          if (!Ext.isEmpty(cmp))
            cmp.hide();
        }
      },
      {
        text: 'Add',
        ui: 'confirm',
        handler: function() {
          var cmp = Ext.getCmp('email-id');
          if (!Ext.isEmpty(cmp))
            cmp.show();
          else {
            pnl.add({
              xtype: 'emailfield',
              id: 'email-id',
              name : 'email',
              label: 'E-mail'
            });
```

```
        pnl.addDocked({
          xtype : 'toolbar',
          dock: 'top',
          items: [{
            text: 'Dummy'
          }]
        });
        pnl.doLayout();
      }
    }
  }
]
}
]
```

See also

▶ The recipe named *Setting up the browser-based development environment* in *Chapter 1*

▶ The recipe named *Working with panel* in this chapter

▶ The recipe named *Panel docking using DockLayout* in this chapter

Building wizards using CardLayout

This recipe describes how to use a card layout as a container layout. Card layout lays items in the form of (playing) cards and shows only one item at a time. We will implement a wizard application to understand the usage of this layout.

Getting ready

Make sure that you have set up your development environment by following the recipes outlined in *Chapter 1*.

How to do it...

Carry out the following steps:

1. Create and open a new file named ch03_04.js and paste the following code into it:

```
Ext.setup({
    onReady: function() {

    var navigate = function(panel, direction){
```

```
        var layout = panel.getLayout();
        layout[direction]();
        Ext.getCmp('move-prev').setDisabled(!layout.getPrev());
        Ext.getCmp('move-next').setDisabled(!layout.getNext());
};

var pnl = new Ext.Panel({
    title: 'Wizard',
    fullscreen: true,
    layout: 'card',
    bodyStyle: 'padding:15px',
    defaults: {
        border: false
    },
    dockedItems: [
      {
            dock : 'top',
            xtype: 'toolbar',
            ui   : 'light',
            items: [
                {
            id: 'move-prev',
            text: 'Back',
            ui: 'back',
            handler: function(btn) {
                navigate(btn.up("panel"), "prev");
            },
            disabled: true
        },{xtype: 'spacer'},
        {
            id: 'move-next',
            text: 'Next',
            ui: 'forward',
            handler: function(btn) {
                navigate(btn.up("panel"), "next");
            }
        }
            ]
        }

    ],
    items: [{
        id: 'card-0',
```

```
            html: '<h1>Welcome to the Wizard!</h1><p>Step 1 of
                  3</p>'
        },{
            id: 'card-1',
            html: '<p>Step 2 of 3</p>'
        },{
            id: 'card-2',
            html: '<h1>Congratulations!</h1><p>Step 3 of 3 -
                  Complete</p>'
        }]
    });
    }
});
```

2. Update the `index.html` file.

3. Deploy and access it from the browser. You will see the following screens when you click on the **Next** button:

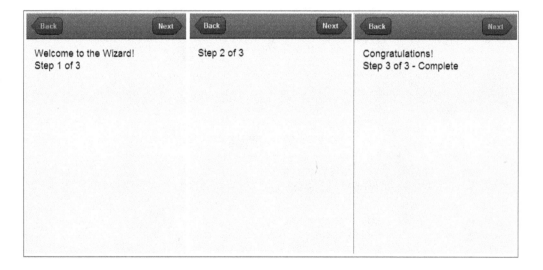

How it works...

The preceding code creates a panel with three child panels and a dock panel with two buttons, **Back** and **Next**. The `layout: 'card'` indicates that the card layout will be used to lay out the panel and its items.

The `navigation` function based on the specified `direction` enables and disables the appropriate panel.

```
var navigate = function(panel, direction){
    var layout = panel.getLayout();
    layout[direction]();
    Ext.getCmp('move-prev').setDisabled(!layout.getPrev());
    Ext.getCmp('move-next').setDisabled(!layout.getNext());
};
```

`panel.getLayout()` returns the `CardLayout` instance, which contains `next()` and `prev()` methods that can set the active panel based on the card stack and the direction. `layout[direction]` calls `next()` or `prev()` depending on the `direction`. Other two lines:

```
Ext.getCmp('move-prev').setDisabled(!layout.getPrev());
Ext.getCmp('move-next').setDisabled(!layout.getNext());
```

In these lines, we are disabling the **Back** button if we have reached the first panel, otherwise it remains enabled. Similarly, for the **Next** button, we will disable it if we have reached the last panel

The button handler calls the `navigate` method where it passes the reference of the panel object (`btn.up("panel")`) and the `direction` text—next using the following line:

```
navigate(btn.up("panel"), "next");
```

There's more...

By default, card layout sets the first item as the active item and the user would see that on the screen when the application comes up. However, there might be a situation where we would like a different item to remain active, by default. Let's see what facility the card layout provides.

Changing the default active item

Card layout provides the property named `activeItem` that can be used to set the item which will be active, by default. The default value of this property is `0`. To show the second item as the default panel when the container is initialized, setting `activeItem` to `1` on the container panel would do the work for us. The following code snippet shows the use of this property:

```
var pnl = new Ext.Panel({
    title: 'Wizard',
    fullscreen: true,
    layout: 'card',
    activeItem: 1,
});
```

Alternatively, you may use the `setActiveItem` method to set the active item at runtime.

See also

▶ The recipe named *Setting up the browser-based development environment* in *Chapter 1*

▶ The recipe named *Working with panel* in this chapter

▶ The recipe named *Panel docking using DockLayout* in this chapter

Panel docking using DockLayout

The dock panel is used to position the child content along the edge of a layout container. Sencha Touch provides the mechanism to dock items along any of the four edges: top, left, bottom, and right. In this recipe, we will see what needs to be done to use a dock layout.

Getting ready

Make sure that you have set up your development environment by following the recipes outlined in *Chapter 1*.

How to do it...

Carry out the following steps:

1. Create and open a new file named ch03_05.js and paste the following code into it:

```
Ext.setup({
    onReady: function() {

    var pnl = new Ext.Panel({
        fullscreen: true,
        bodyStyle: 'padding:15px',
        dockedItems: [{
          dock : 'top',
            bodyStyle: 'background:grey;',
            html: '<p>Panel 1</p>'
        },{
          dock : 'bottom',
            bodyStyle: 'background:blue;',
            html: '<p>Panel 2</p>'
        },{
          dock : 'right',
            bodyStyle: 'background:green;',
            html: '<p>Panel 3</p>'
        },{
```

```
            dock : 'left',
              bodyStyle: 'background:yellow;',
              html: '<p>Panel 4</p>'
        }]
    });
      }
    });
```

2. Update the `index.html` file.

3. Deploy and access it from the browser. The following screenshot shows how the view will look:

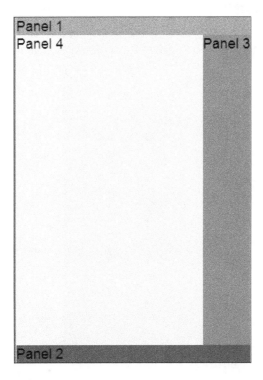

How it works...

The preceding code creates a panel with four docking panels along four different edges. The dock layout considers the `dockedItems` property. In addition, irrespective of the value of the `layout` config, if a container has `dockedItems` defined, they would be rendered using the `dock` layout.

Dock is a property specific to the dock layout. By default, the dock layout will render the item at the top if the dock property is not set for that item.

See also

▸ The recipe named *Setting up the browser-based development environment* in *Chapter 1*

▸ The recipe named *Working with panel* in this chapter

Fitting into the container using FitLayout

The fit layout is for the container that contains a single item that automatically expands to fill the layout's container. The card layout utilizes the fit layout to fit an item into a card. In this recipe, we will learn about the use of the fit layout.

Getting ready

Make sure that you have set up your development environment by following the recipes outlined in *Chapter 1*.

How to do it...

Carry out the following steps:

1. Create and open a new file named ch03_06.js and paste the following code into it:

```
Ext.setup({
    onReady: function() {

    var pnl = new Ext.Panel({
        fullscreen: true,
        layout: 'fit',
        bodyStyle: 'padding:15px',
        items: [{
            bodyStyle: 'background:grey;',
            html: '<p>Panel 1</p>'
        }]
    });
    }
});
```

2. Update the index.html file.

3. Deploy and access it from the browser. The following screenshot shows the view:

How it works...

`layout: 'fit'` initializes the fit layout class and associates it with the panel, which will then be used to render the child items. There is no other config specific to the fit layout.

 If the container with a fit layout has multiple panels, then only the first one will be displayed.

See also

▸ The recipe named _Setting up the browser-based development environment_ in _Chapter 1_

▸ The recipe named _Working with panel_ in this chapter

Arranging your items horizontally using HBoxLayout

The HBox layout arranges items horizontally across a container. It optionally divides the available horizontal space between child items containing a `flex` configuration, which is numeric. The `flex` option is a ratio that distributes the width after any items with explicit widths have been accounted for. We can either use the `width` property to specify a fixed width or use `flex`. This recipe describes how we can arrange our items using the `hbox` layout.

Getting ready

Make sure that you have set up your development environment by following the recipes outlined in *Chapter 1*.

How to do it...

Carry out the following steps:

1. Create and open a new file named `ch03_07.js` and paste the following code into it:

```
Ext.setup({
    onReady: function() {
  var pnl = new Ext.Panel({
        width: 400,
        height: 300,
        fullscreen: true,
        layout: 'hbox',
        items: [{
            flex: 3,
            html: 'First',
            bodyStyle: 'background:grey;'
        },{
            width: 100,
            html: 'Second',
            bodyStyle: 'background:blue;'
        },{
            flex: 2,
            html: 'Third',
            bodyStyle: 'background:yellow;'
        }]
    });
    }
});
```

2. Update the `index.html` file.

3. Deploy and access it from the browser. The following screenshot shows the view:

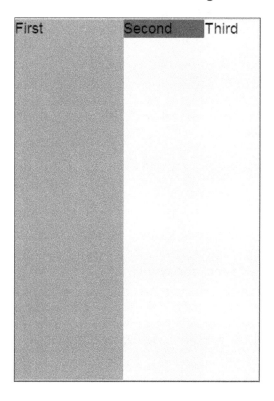

How it works...

The preceding code creates a panel 400 pixels wide and 300 pixels high. In addition, it has three child panels where one panel has a fixed width of 100px and others are using flex. This is how the `hbox` layout will calculate the width of each item:

▶   The fixed width item is subtracted, leaving us with 300px width

▶   The total flex number is counted, in this case, it is 5

▶   The ratio is then calculated, 300 / 5 = 60

▶   The first item has a flex of 3, so its width is set to 3 * 60 = 180px

▶   The other remaining item is set to 2 * 60 = 120px

There's more...

Additionally, the `hbox` layout provides options such as rendering the items in the reverse order, and controlling the vertical and horizontal alignment of the item.

Component vertical alignment

If there is no height specified for the items, you would notice that the items do not occupy the complete container height. In some cases, you may have a need to make the item occupy the complete container height. In order to achieve this, set the `align` property to `stretch`, as shown in the following code snippet:

```
layout: {
        type: 'hbox',
        align: 'stretch'
}
```

Other valid values for the align property are `center`, `start`, and `end`.

Lay out items in reverse order

Suppose we are developing a panel where, based on the user locale, you may want to show the items from left-to-right or right-to-left. If this is a need, then we can use the `direction` property to achieve the desired result. Setting the `direction` to `reverse` would render the items in the reverse order. The following code snippet shows the use of the property:

```
layout: {
        type: 'hbox',
        direction: 'reverse'
}
```

Once set, the view will show the panels in the reverse order as shown in the following screenshot:

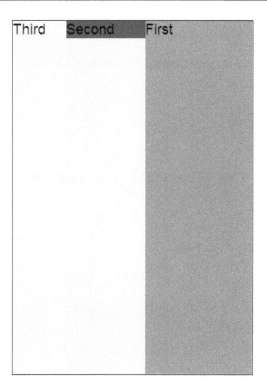

See also

▶ The recipe named *Setting up the browser-based development environment* in *Chapter 1*

▶ The recipe named *Working with panel* in this chapter

Arranging your items vertically using VBoxLayout

The VBox layout arranges items vertically down in a container. It optionally divides the available vertical space between child items containing a `flex` configuration, which is numeric. The `flex` option is a ratio that distributes the height after any items with explicit heights have been accounted for. We can either use the `height` property to specify a fixed height or use `flex`. This recipe describes how we can arrange our items by using the `vbox` layout.

Getting ready

Make sure that you have set up your development environment by following the recipes outlined in *Chapter 1*.

How to do it...

Carry out the following steps:

1. Create and open a new file named `ch03_08.js` and paste the following code into it:

```
Ext.setup({
    onReady: function() {

    var pnl = new Ext.Panel({
        width: 400,
        height: 400,
        fullscreen: true,
        layout: {
            type: 'vbox',
            align: 'stretch'
        },
        items: [{
            flex: 2,
            html: 'First',
            bodyStyle: 'background:grey;'
        },{
            height: 100,
            html: 'Second',
            bodyStyle: 'background:blue;'
        },{
            flex: 1,
            html: 'Third',
            bodyStyle: 'background:yellow;'
        }]
    });
    }
});
```

2. Update the `index.html` file.
3. Deploy and access it from the browser. The following screenshot shows the view:

How it works...

The preceding code creates a panel 400 pixels wide and 400 pixels high. In addition, it has three child panels where one panel has a fixed height of 100px and the others are using flex. This is how the vbox layout will calculate the height of each item:

 ▸ The fixed height item is subtracted, leaving us with a 300px height

 ▸ The total flex number is counted, in this case, it is 3

 ▸ The ratio is then calculated, 300 / 3 = 100

 ▸ The first item has a flex of 2, so its height is set to 2 * 100 = 200px

 ▸ The other remaining item is set to 1 * 100 = 100px

- ▸ The recipe named *Setting up the browser-based development environment* in *Chapter 1*
- ▸ The recipe named *Working with panel* in this chapter

Mixing layouts

In previous recipes, we looked at the different container layouts which are available with Sencha Touch. Given the different layouts, a question that arises is whether these layouts are compatible with each other to an extent where they can be nested. For example, is it valid to use the `hbox` layout at the parent container level but use `vbox` inside the subcontainer? The answer is, Yes. Technically, it is feasible to combine multiple layouts to create complex looking views. For example, we can have a panel with a card layout, with each item having an `hbox` layout and each of its items having a `vbox` layout and the final container having an `auto` layout with few docked items defined.

In this recipe, we will see how we can mix different layouts and the important points that we need to keep in mind when we use these combinations.

Getting ready

Make sure that you have set up your development environment by following the recipes outlined in *Chapter 1*.

How to do it...

Carry out the following steps:

1. Create and open a new file named `ch03_09.js` and paste the following code into it:

```
Ext.setup({
    onReady: function() {
var pnl = new Ext.Panel({
    width: 400,
    height: 400,
    fullscreen: true,
    layout: {
        type: 'vbox',
        align: 'stretch'
    },
    items: [{
        flex: 2,
```

```
            html: 'First',
            bodyStyle: 'background:grey;',
            items: [{layout: {
                type: 'hbox',
                align: 'stretch'
        },
        items: [{
                flex: 2,
                html: 'First',
                bodyStyle: 'background:grey;',
                items: [{layout: 'fit',
        bodyStyle: 'padding:15px',
        items: [{
                    xtype: 'textareafield',
                    name : 'url',
                    label: 'Website'
                }]
            }]
        },{
                width: 100,
                html: 'Second',
                bodyStyle: 'background:blue;'
        },{
                flex: 1,
                html: 'Third',
                bodyStyle: 'background:yellow;'
        }]}]
        },{
                height: 100,
                html: 'Second',
                bodyStyle: 'background:blue;'
        },{
                flex: 1,
                html: 'Third',
                bodyStyle: 'background:yellow;'
        }]
    });
    }
});
```

2. Update the `index.html` file.

3. Deploy and access it from the browser. The following screenshot shows the view:

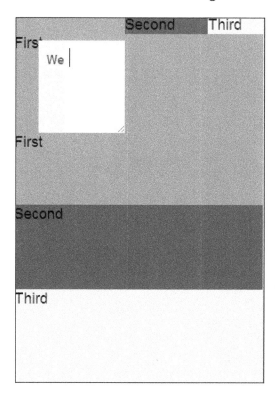

How it works...

The preceding code creates a top-level panel with the vbox layout and one of its items having an hbox layout. The subitem of the panel with the hbox layout has an item with the fit layout.

See also

▶ The recipe named *Setting up the browser-based development environment* in *Chapter 1*

▶ The recipe named *Working with panel* in this chapter

4
Building Custom Views

In this chapter, we will cover:

- ▶ Basic HTML templating using Template
- ▶ Using XTemplate for advanced templating
- ▶ Conditional view rendering using XTemplate
- ▶ Designing a custom view using DataView
- ▶ Showing the filtered data
- ▶ Responding to the user action

Introduction

In *Chapters 2* and *3*, we saw how to make use of different form fields, containers, and layouts to create a view of our choice. The out-of-the-box layouts provided by Sencha Touch have a pre-defined way to position the components and calculate their sizes. Often, there may be situations in the application where the view cannot be created, directly using the available containers, components, and layouts. For example, if we wanted to create a photo album where the view shows the photos in a matrix based on the dimension of the device. Alternatively, suppose we wanted to design a view similar to the Facebook feed view. There is no direct layout supporting these needs. If we try to achieve it by mixing different layouts, it would become a heavy view, which would use multiple containers. We would have to work with the styles to do some tweaking on top of what the layouts provide us to align the information properly. Alternatively, Sencha Touch provides us a way to create templates using HTML fragments and use them along with the data set to render custom views.

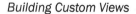

There are two types of templates provided: **Template** and **XTemplate**. Template provides us the basic template functionality, whereas XTemplate is much more advanced. Additionally, Sencha Touch provides a **DataView**, which uses an XTemplate to render the view and a store for the data. It also provides events which can be used to respond to user actions.

In this chapter, we will learn about each one of these options to render the custom view and understand their specific usage.

Basic HTML templating using Template

Template provides a way to create templates using the HTML fragments. It contains HTML elements and various placeholders which are replaced with the values of the fields present in the data that is given to the template API to use in conjunction with the template text. For example, we may have a <div> element present in the body and, based on the data, we may add <ul> and <li> elements to it at runtime.

In this recipe, we will look at a typical usage of template and understand what it takes to define and use one.

Getting ready

Make sure that you have set up your development environment by following the *Gear up for the Journey* recipe outlined in *Chapter 1*.

Create a new folder named ch04 in the same folder where we created the ch01 and ch02 folders. We will be using this new folder in which to keep the code.

How to do it...

Carry out the following steps:

1. Create and open a new file named ch04_01.js and paste the following code into it:

```
Ext.setup({
  onReady: function() {

    var data = [{
        album:'rose',
        url:'http://www.pictures.vg/vgflowers/400x300/flowers_
          pics_4870.jpg',
        title:'Rose 1',
        about:'Peach'}, {
        album:'rose',
        url:'http://www.pictures.vg/vgflowers/400x300/
          redroses08.jpg',
```

```
title:'Rose 2',
about:'Red'}, {
album:'rose',
url:'http://www.pictures.vg/vgflowers/400x300/
   abflowers5613.jpg',
title:'Rose 3',
about:'Pink'}, {
album:'rose',
url:'http://www.pictures.vg/vgflowers/400x300/
   cflowers0399.jpg',
title:'Rose 4',
about:'Orange'}, {
album:'daffodil',
url:'http://www.pictures.vg/vgflowers/400x300/
   daff001.jpg',
title:'Daffodil 1',
about:'Yellow'}, {
album:'daffodil',
url:'http://www.pictures.vg/vgflowers/400x300/
   cflowers0484.jpg',
title:'Daffodil 2',
about:'Small'}, {
album:'daffodil',
url:'http://www.pictures.vg/vgflowers/400x300/
   abflowers2232.jpg',
title:'Daffodil 2',
about:'Orange'}, {
album:'daffodil',
url:'http://www.pictures.vg/vgflowers/400x300/
   abflowers7230.jpg',
title:'Daffodil 2',
about:'Winter'}, {
album:'hibiscus',
url:'http://www.pictures.vg/vgflowers/400x300/
   cflowers4214.jpg',
title:'Hibiscus 1',
about:'Peach'}, {
album:'hibiscus',
url:'http://www.pictures.vg/vgflowers/400x300/
   cflowers3250.jpg',
title:'Hibiscus 1',
about:'Red'}, {
album:'hibiscus',
url:'http://www.pictures.vg/vgflowers/400x300/
   cflowers2631.jpg',
```

```
              title:'Hibiscus 1',
              about:'Pink'}, {
            album:'hibiscus',
            url:'http://www.pictures.vg/vgflowers/400x300/
              cflowers5645.jpg',
            title:'Hibiscus 1',
            about:'Maroon'}, {
            album:'hibiscus',
            url:'http://www.pictures.vg/vgflowers/400x300/
              cflowers0577.jpg',
            title:'Hibiscus 1',
            about:'Pink'}, {
            album:'hibiscus',
            url:'http://www.pictures.vg/vgflowers/400x300/
              cflowers3224.jpg',
            title:'Hibiscus 1',
            about:'Bright Red'}];

    var t = new Ext.Template
      ('<div style="float:left;margin:10px;border:solid;">',
      '<img border="0" src={url} title={title} width="100"
        height="80" />',
                '<p>{about}</p>',
              '</div>');

    Ext.each(data, function(item, index, allItems){
      t.append(Ext.getBody(), item);
    });
    }
  });
```

2. Update the index.html file.

3. Deploy and access it from the browser. You may also run it using the emulator. You will see a screen similar to the one shown in the following screenshot:

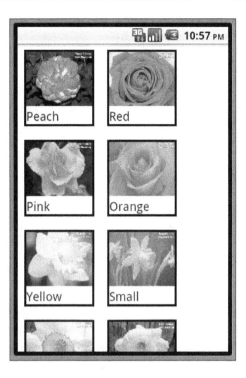

How it works...

In the preceding code, we have a JSON object stored in `data`. Each data has `album`, `url`, `title`, and `about` fields which are referred to in the HTML fragment given to the template.

```
{
    album:'rose',
    url:'http://www.pictures.vg/vgflowers/400x300/
        flowers_pics_4870.jpg',
    title:'Rose 1',
    about:'Peach'

}
```

The following code instantiates `Ext.Template` with the HTML fragment containing the placeholders: {url}, {title}, {about}, which are then replaced with the real values from the data when the `append` method is called on the template. The placeholder name must match with the field name in the data.

```
var t = new Ext.Template
    ('<div style="float:left;margin:10px;border:solid;">',
    '<img border="0" src={url} title={title} width="100"
        height="80" />',
```

```
'<p>{about}</p>',
'</div>');
```

In the following code, we are calling the template's `append` method to render each item to the body:

```
Ext.each(data, function(item, index, allItems){
    t.append(Ext.getBody(), item);
});
```

There's more...

A template uses placeholders, which can be either a field name or an index in the data. Internally, a template goes through the stage of compilation and then starts applying the data to the template to get the final HTML fragment that is appended to the element (in this case, `body`). Additionally, it also provides us a way to use different in-built formats and apply them to the data before displaying.

Compiling the template

Compilation of a template is a costly affair. This is the stage where the framework parses the template string and replaces the appropriate function references to get the values for the placeholders. If we are creating a template once in our code and re-using it to render a view at different stages in the code, then it makes sense to minimize the time spent in the compilation because now the template can be compiled only once and used multiple times. `Ext.Template` provides the option as well as a method to compile the template. The property named `compiled`, when set to `true` at the time of instantiating a template, will be instantiated and then compiled. However, on-demand, if we want to compile the template, then we can call the `compile` method on the template instance. The following code snippet shows the use of the property for an immediate compilation:

```
var t = new Ext.Template
  ('<div style="float:left;margin:10px;border:solid;">',
  '<img border="0" src={url} title={title} width="100"
     height="80" />',
  '<p>{about}</p>',
  '</div>',
  {
    compiled: true    // compile immediately

  }
);
```

The following code snippet shows the usage of the `compile` method:

```
t.compile();
```

Formatting values

In some cases, there may be a need to cook the incoming data before it is displayed on the screen. For example, you may want to format the date properly or you may want to terminate the large text with ellipsis. The `Ext.Template` class allows us to use the formats defined in the `Ext.util.Format` class to format the values. The following code snippet shows a typical usage of a format:

```
var t = new Ext.Template([
  '<div name="{id}">',
  '<span class="{cls}">{name:trim} {value:ellipsis(10)}</span>',
  '</div>',
]);
```

See also

The recipe named *Setting up the browser-based development environment* in *Chapter 1*

Using XTemplate for advanced templating

Conceptually, XTemplate provides similar functionality to that which Template provides. However, it also provides certain advanced functionalities to work with the template and its data quickly. This recipe describes the use of XTemplate and demonstrates the difference between XTemplate and Template.

Getting ready

Make sure that you have set up your development environment by following the recipes outlined in *Chapter 1*.

How to do it...

Carry out the following steps:

1. Create and open a new file named `ch04_02.js` and paste the following code into it:

```
Ext.setup({
    onReady: function() {

        var data = [{
        album:'rose',
        url:'http://www.pictures.vg/vgflowers/400x300/
          flowers_pics_4870.jpg',
        title:'Rose 1',
        about:'Peach'},

            ...

            ...
    {
        album:'hibiscus',
        url:'http:/
        /www.pictures.vg/vgflowers/400x300/cflowers2631.jpg',
        title:'Hibiscus 1',
        about:'Pink'}];

        var t = new Ext.XTemplate('<tpl for=".">',
          '<div style="float:left;margin:10px;border:solid;">',
            '<img border="0" src={url} title={title} width="100"
              height="80" />',
            '<p>{about}</p>',
          '</div></tpl>');
        t.append(Ext.getBody(), data);
    }
});
```

2. Update the `index.html` file.

3. Deploy and access it from the browser. You may also run it using the emulator. You will see a screen similar to the one shown in the following screenshot:

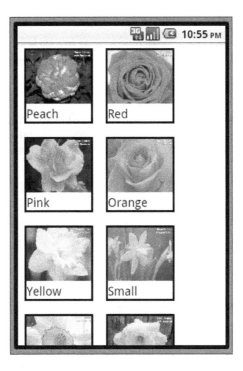

How it works...

The preceding code uses the same JSON data that we used in the previous recipe.

We are then instantiating the `Ext.XTemplate` class with a similar HTML fragment, which we used with the `Ext.Template`:

```
var t = new Ext.XTemplate('<tpl for=".">',
   '<div style="float:left;margin:10px;border:solid;">',
   '<img border="0" src={url} title={title} width="100"
      height="80" />',
               '<p>{about}</p>',
            '</div></tpl>');
```

One difference is that, now, in the HTML fragment, we have enclosed the original HTML within a `<tpl>` tag, which is specific to the `XTemplate`. `<tpl for=".">` is an `XTemplate` shortcut to say that this HTML fragment will be used for each item in the `data` array, which is passed to the template `append` method. As the looping construct is part of the `XTemplate`, we don't have to loop through the `data` array. So, the `t.append(Ext.getBody(), data);` line will do the work for us.

Similar to `Ext.Template`, `Ext.XTemplate` also provides the compilation and formatting capabilities.

Compiling the template

`XTemplate` also has a property named `compiled` and a method `compile` to accomplish the compilation task. The following code snippet shows the use of the property for immediate compilation:

```
var t = new Ext.XTemplate
  ('<div style="float:left;margin:10px;border:solid;">',
    '<img border="0" src={url} title={title} width="100"
      height="80" />',
    '<p>{about}</p>',
    '</div>',
  {
    compiled: true    // compile immediately
  }
);
```

The following code snippet shows the usage of the `compile` method:

```
t.compile();
```

Formatting values

`XTemplate` has similar formatting functionality that is available with `Template`. Refer to the *Basic HTML templating using Template* recipe for more details.

- ▶ The recipe named *Setting up the browser-based development environment* in *Chapter 1*
- ▶ The recipe named *Basic HTML templating using Template* in this chapter

Conditional view rendering using XTemplate

In the previous recipe, we saw how to use XTemplate, but did not utilize its capabilities such as using auto-filling arrays, conditional processing, math function, and so on to build the view by making different decisions on the incoming data. For example, in the previous recipe, we are showing all kinds of flowers in our view. What if we just want to show roses? This is where XTemplate helps us to put the constructs inside the template definition and not make any change to the data.

Getting ready

Make sure that you have set up your development environment by following the recipes outlined in *Chapter 1*.

How to do it...

Carry out the following steps:

1. Create and open a new file named ch04_03.js and paste the following code into it:

```
Ext.setup({
    onReady: function() {

        var data = [{
        album:'rose',
        url:'http://www.pictures.vg/vgflowers/400x300/
          flowers_pics_4870.jpg',
        title:'Rose 1',
        about:'Peach'},
          ...
          ...
    {
        album:'hibiscus',
        url:'http://www.pictures.vg/vgflowers/400x300/
          cflowers2631.jpg',
        title:'Hibiscus 1',
        about:'Pink'}];
        var t = new Ext.XTemplate('<tpl>',
            '<tpl for="items">',
            '<tpl if="album==parent.filter && this.
              matchFound()">',
            '<div style="float:left;margin:10px;border:sol
              id;">',
```

```
        '<img border="0" src={url} title={title}
          width="100" height="80" />',
          '<p>{about}</p>',
        '</div></tpl></tpl>',
        '<tpl if="this.isMatchNotFound()">',
        '<h1>No match found!!',
        '</tpl></tpl>',
        {
          found: false,
          matchFound: function(){
            this.found = true;
            return this.found;
          },
          isMatchNotFound: function(){
            return this.found ? false: true;
          }
        });

    t.append(Ext.getBody(), {filter: 'rose', items: data});
  }
});
```

2. Update the `index.html` file.

3. Deploy and access it from the browser. You may also run it using the emulator. You will see a screen similar to the one shown in the following screenshot:

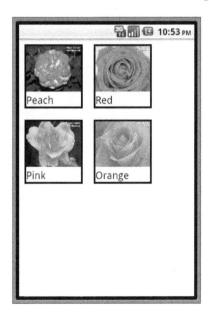

How it works...

The preceding code uses the additional capabilities such as conditions, loops, inline functions, and in-built variables offered by XTemplate to show the filtered items. Based on the value specified in the filter property of the data, which is passed to the template, it checks if there are images whose album name matches with the filter and the matching ones are shown in the view, otherwise the No match found! message is displayed.

The data, which is being passed to the template, has the following structure:

```
{filter: 'rose', items: data}
```

<tpl for="items"> tells that the content inside this <tpl> tag is applied to each item of the items array passed as part of the data.

In the line:

```
<tpl if="album==parent.filter && this.matchFound()">
```

We are comparing the album field on the incoming data with the filter value ('rose' in this case) and calling an inline function matchFound() to set a member property found to true indicating that a matching item has been found, as shown in the following code:

```
matchFound: function(){
       this.found = true;
       return this.found;
}
```

For the entire matching item, the following HTML fragment is used to render them:

```
'<div style="float:left;margin:10px;border:solid;">',
  '<img border="0" src={url} title={title} width="100"
      height="80" />',
  '<p>{about}</p>',
  '</div>'
```

The following template fragment checks if there are any matches found; if no, it displays No match found!!:

```
'<tpl if="this.isMatchNotFound()">',
            '<h1>No match found!!',
            '</tpl>
```

The recipe named *Setting up the browser-based development environment* in *Chapter 1.*

Designing a custom view using DataView

`Template` and `XTemplate` provide a way to create elements using the template, placeholders, and the data. There is one thing which is not really straightforward and this is the support for events. For example, if you want to handle the click on a rose to show a bigger picture of it, this is not very straightforward. We will have to work with elements and register handlers for the different DOM events that we may be interested in. In addition, there is no way to leverage the store. Store is covered in more detail in the next chapter. For now, we can say that a store is a data structure, which can hold a collection of records and can be associated with components, such as DataView, to provide it the required data to render their view. Sencha Touch provides a convenient way to create views by using `XTemplate` and link it with a data store and also provides events that we can handle to respond to the user action—using `DataView`.

This recipe describes the steps to use `DataView`.

Getting ready

Make sure that you have set up your development environment by following the recipes outlined in *Chapter 1.*

How to do it...

Carry out the following steps:

1. Create and open a new file named `ch04_04.js` and paste the following code into it:

```
Ext.setup({
    onReady: function() {

    var data = [{
        album:'rose',
        url:'http://www.pictures.vg/vgflowers/400x300/
          flowers_pics_4870.jpg',
        title:'Rose 1',
        about:'Peach'}
        ...
        ...
    , {
```

```
                album:'hibiscus',
                url:'http://www.pictures.vg/vgflowers/400x300/
                  cflowers2631.jpg',
                title:'Hibiscus 1',
                about:'Pink'}];

        var store = new Ext.data.JsonStore({
            data: data,
            mode: 'local',
            fields: [
                'url', 'title','about'
            ]
        });

        var tpl = new Ext.XTemplate(
            '<tpl for=".">',
                '<div class="thumb-wrap" id="{title}">',
                '<div class="thumb"><img src="{url}" title="{title}">
                  </div>',
                '<span class="x-editable">{about}</span></div>',
            '</tpl>',
            '<div class="x-clear"></div>'
        );
        var panel = new Ext.Panel({
            id:'images-view',
            frame:true,
            width:535,
            fullscreen: true,
            autoHeight:true,
            layout:'fit',
            title:'Simple DataView',

            items: new Ext.DataView({
                data: data,
                store: store,
                tpl: tpl,
                autoHeight:true,
                overItemCls:'x-view-over',
                itemSelector:'div.thumb-wrap',
                emptyText: 'No images to display'
            })
        });
    }
});
```

2. Create and open a new file named `ch04.css` and paste the following style code into it:

```css
#images-view .x-panel-body{
  background: white;
  font: 11px Arial, Helvetica, sans-serif;
}
#images-view .thumb{
  background: #dddddd;
  padding: 3px;
}
#images-view .thumb img{
  height: 60px;
  width: 80px;
}
#images-view .thumb-wrap{
  float: left;
  margin: 4px;
  margin-right: 0;
  padding: 5px;
}
#images-view .thumb-wrap span{
  display: block;
  overflow: hidden;
  text-align: center;
}

#images-view .x-view-over{
  border:1px solid #dddddd;
  background: #efefef url(images/row-over.gif) repeat-x left top;
  padding: 4px;
}

#images-view .x-item-selected{
  background: #eff5fb url(images/selected.gif)
    no-repeat right bottom;
  border:1px solid #99bbe8;
  padding: 4px;
}
#images-view .x-item-selected .thumb{
  background:transparent;
}
```

3. Update the `index.html` file by including the css and js files.

4. Deploy and access it from the browser. You may also run it using the emulator. You will see a screen similar to the one shown in the following screenshot:

How it works...

The preceding code uses the `Ext.DataView` class to create a custom view. We have created a panel with `DataView` as its child item.

First, we created a JSON store to hold the data. You may refer to *Chapter 5, Dealing with Data and Data Sources* for a detailed discussion on the different type of stores:

```
var store = new Ext.data.JsonStore({
    data: data,
    mode: 'local',
    fields: [
        'url', 'title','about'
    ]
});
```

`url`, `title`, and `about` are the fields that will be present in the record stored within the `store`. `mode: 'local'` tells us that the data for the store is coming from the in-memory object rather than from a remote location.

Then, we instantiated `XTemplate` in the following part of the code:

```
var tpl = new Ext.XTemplate(
  '<tpl for=".">',
    '<div class="thumb-wrap" id="{title}">',
    '<div class="thumb"><img src="{url}" title="{title}"></div>',
    '<span class="x-editable">{about}</span></div>',
  '</tpl>',
  '<div class="x-clear"></div>'
);
```

The template is using `title`, `url`, and `about` as the placeholders. The CSS classes used in the template are defined in the `ch04.css` file.

Next, we created a panel with the `fit` layout and `DataView` as its only item, so that it fits itself to the area available with the container panel.

To the panel, we are adding `DataView` as follows:

```
items: new Ext.DataView({
        data: data,
        store: store,
        tpl: tpl,
        autoHeight:true,
        overItemCls:'x-view-over',
        itemSelector:'div.thumb-wrap',
        emptyText: 'No images to display'
})
```

`store: store` is where we associated our store object with `DataView`. Moreover, the `tpl` property helps us in associating `XTemplate` with `DataView`, which it will use to render the items in the view. `itemSelector` tells that when the user selects or taps, the element accessible using the `div.thumb-wrap` selector will be returned to the event handlers.

There's more...

When we are working with custom views, it is also important that we are sensitive towards the orientation change. Let's see how it can be done with `DataView`.

Orientation change

In order to handle the orientation change, first we will have to set the `monitorOrientation` property to `true` on `DataView` and register a handler for the `orientationchange` event on `DataView` and in the handler; we must call the `refresh` method. The following code snippet shows how to do this:

```
orientationchange: function(thisPnl, orientation, width, height) {
  thisPnl.refresh();
}
```

See also

▸ The recipe named *Setting up the browser-based development environment* in *Chapter 1*

▸ The recipe named *Working with Panel* in *Chapter 3*

▸ The recipe named *Working with Store* in *Chapter 5*

Showing the filtered data

In the previous recipe, we saw how to create `DataView` and use `XTemplate` and a store to generate the view. In this recipe, we will see if we have to show only the relevant items in the view, and how we go about approaching it.

Getting ready

Make sure that you have set up your development environment by following the recipes outlined in *Chapter 1*.

How to do it...

Carry out the following steps:

1. Create and open a new file named `ch04_05.js` and paste the following code into it:

```
Ext.setup({
    onReady: function() {

    var data = [{
        album:'rose',
        url:'http://www.pictures.vg/vgflowers/400x300/
          flowers_pics_4870.jpg',
        title:'Rose 1',
        about:'Peach'},
```

```
        ...
        ...
, {
        album:'hibiscus',
        url:'http://www.pictures.vg/vgflowers/400x300/
          cflowers3224.jpg',
        title:'Hibiscus 1',
        about:'Bright Red'}];

var store = new Ext.data.JsonStore({
    data: data,
    mode: 'local',
    fields: [
        'url', 'title','about'
    ]
});

var tpl = new Ext.XTemplate(
  '<tpl for=".">',
    '<div class="thumb-wrap" id="{title}">',
    '<div class="thumb"><img src="{url}"
      title="{title}"></div>',
    '<span>{about}</span></div>',
  '</tpl>',
  '<div class="x-clear"></div>'
);


var filter = function(criteria) {
return store.filterBy(function(record, id){
                if (record.get('album') === criteria ||
                  Ext.isEmpty(criteria))
                    return true;
                else
                    return false;
            });
}

var pnl = new Ext.Panel({
  id:'images-view',
    fullscreen: true,
    defaults: {
        border: false
    },
```

```
    items: new Ext.DataView({
        data: data,
        store: store,
        tpl: tpl,
        autoHeight:true,
        simpleSelect: true,
        overItemCls:'x-view-over',
        itemSelector:'div.thumb-wrap',
        emptyText: 'No images to display'
    }),
    dockedItems: [
        {
            xtype: 'toolbar',
            dock: 'top',
            items: [
                {
                    text: 'Rose',
                    handler: function() {
                        filter('rose');
                    }
                },
                {
                    text: 'Daffodil',
                    handler: function() {
                      filter('daffodil');
                    }
                },{
                    text: 'Hibiscus',
                    handler: function() {
                        filter('hibiscus');
                    }
                },{
                    text: 'Reset',
                    ui: 'confirm',
                    handler: function() {
                        filter('');
                    }
                }
            ]
        }
    ]
});
    }
});
```

2. Update the `index.html` file.

3. Deploy and access it from the browser. You may also run it using the emulator. You will see a screen similar to the one shown in the following screenshot:

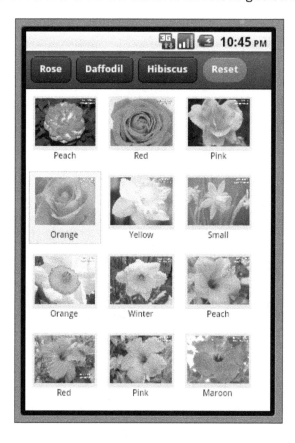

4. Click on the **Rose** button. You will see roses on the screen as shown in the following screenshot:

How it works...

In the preceding code, besides `DataView`, we have also added a docked toolbar with a button for each album (**Rose**, **Daffodil**, and **Hibiscus**) and a **Reset** button. We have then registered the click handler for all buttons and each handler is calling the `filter` function with the filter criteria as follows:

```
{
    text: 'Hibiscus',
    handler: function() {
        filter('hibiscus');
    }
}
```

In the case of the **Reset** click handler, `filter('')` is called which ensures that all the items are displayed in the view as shown in the following code snippet:

```
var filter = function(criteria) {
    return store.filterBy(function(record, id){
        if (record.get('album') === criteria || Ext.isEmpty(criteria))
            return true;
```

```
    else
      return false;
  });
}
```

See also

▶ The recipe named *Setting up the browser-based development environment* in *Chapter 1*

▶ The recipe named *Working with Panel* in *Chapter 3*

▶ The recipe named *Designing a custom view using DataView* in this chapter

▶ The recipe named *Working with Store* in *Chapter 5*

▶ The recipe named *Filtering data* in *Chapter 5*

Responding to the user action

So far, we have seen how to create DataView, bind it to an XTemplate and a store, and apply certain filtering on the data. In this recipe, we will see how to handle the events generated as part of the user action, for example, when a user selects an item in the view.

Getting ready

Make sure that you have set up your development environment by following the recipes outlined in *Chapter 1*.

How to do it...

Carry out the following steps:

1. Create and open a new file named ch04_06.js and paste the following code into it:

```
Ext.setup({
    onReady: function() {

    var data = [{
        album:'rose',
        url:'http://www.pictures.vg/vgflowers/400x300/
          flowers_pics_4870.jpg',
        title:'Rose 1',
        about:'Peach'},
        …
        …
```

```
,{
        album:'hibiscus',
        url:'http://www.pictures.vg/vgflowers/400x300/
          cflowers3224.jpg',
        title:'Hibiscus 1',
        about:'Bright Red'}];

var store = new Ext.data.JsonStore({
    data: data,
    mode: 'local',
    fields: [
        'url', 'title','about'
    ]
});

var tpl = new Ext.XTemplate(
 '<tpl for=".">',
   '<div class="thumb-wrap" id="{title}">',
   '<div class="thumb"><img src="{url}" title="{title}"></div>',
   '<span>{about}</span></div>',
 '</tpl>',
 '<div class="x-clear"></div>'
);



var filter = function(criteria) {
return store.filterBy(function(record, id){
  if (record.get('album') === criteria || Ext.isEmpty(criteria))
    return true;
  else
    return false;
  });
}


var pnl = new Ext.Panel({
  id:'images-view',
    fullscreen: true,
    scroll: false,
    monitorOrientation: true,
    layout: 'card',
    defaults: {
        border: false
    },
```

```
items: [new Ext.DataView({
  data: data,
  store: store,
  scroll: 'vertical',
  tpl: tpl,
  autoHeight:true,
  singleSelect: true,
  overItemCls:'x-view-over',
  itemSelector:'div.thumb-wrap',
  emptyText: 'No images to display',
  listeners: {
    selectionchange: function(model, recs) {
      if (recs.length > 0) {
        Ext.getCmp('detail-panel').update('<img src="' +
          recs[0].data.url + '" title="' +
          recs[0].data.title + '">');
        Ext.getCmp('images-view').
          getLayout().setActiveItem(1);
        Ext.getCmp('back-button').show();
        Ext.getCmp('rose-button').hide();
        Ext.getCmp('daffodil-button').hide();
        Ext.getCmp('hibiscus-button').hide();
      }
    }
  }
}), new Ext.Panel({
    id: 'detail-panel',
    width: 400,
    height: 300,
    styleHtmlContent: true,
    scroll: 'vertical',
    cls: 'htmlcontent'
  })],
dockedItems: [
  {
    xtype: 'toolbar',
    dock: 'top',
    items: [
      {
        text: 'Rose',
        id: 'rose-button',
        handler: function() {
          filter('rose');
        }
```

```
            },
            {
              text: 'Daffodil',
              id: 'daffodil-button',
              handler: function() {
                filter('daffodil');
              }
            },{
                text: 'Hibiscus',
                id: 'hibiscus-button',
                handler: function() {
                  filter('hibiscus');
                }
              },{
                  text: 'Reset',
                  id: 'reset-button',
                   ui: 'decline-round',
                   handler: function() {
                      Ext.getCmp('images-view').
                        getLayout().setActiveItem(0);
                      filter('');
                    }
                  },{
                      text: 'Back',
                      id: 'back-button',
                      ui: 'back',
                      hidden: true,
                      handler: function() {
                        Ext.getCmp('images-view').
                          getLayout().setActiveItem(0);
                        this.hide();
                        Ext.getCmp('rose-button').show();
                        Ext.getCmp('daffodil-button').show();
                        Ext.getCmp('hibiscus-button').show();
                      }
                    }
                  ]
                }
            ]
    });

    }
});
```

2. Update the `index.html` file.

3. Deploy and access it from the browser. You may also run it using the emulator. You will see a screen as shown in the following screenshot:

4. Click on an item. You will see the bigger image shown in the second card with the **Reset** and **Back** button on the toolbar, as shown in the following screenshot:

How it works...

The preceding code makes changes on top of the functionality that we built in the previous recipe. We changed the layout of the main container panel from fit to card and added `DataView` to the first card and another panel to the second card to show the bigger image of the selected flower. In addition, we added a `Back` button to the docked toolbar, so that the user can come back to the multiple images view from the detail view.

`singleSelect` is set to `true` on `DataView` to enable the user to select an item from the view. Moreover, a `selectionchange` listener is registered to show the bigger image of the flower on the second card panel, switch the active panel to the second, and show/hide the toolbar buttons, appropriately, as follows:

```
singleSelect: true,
listeners: {
  selectionchange: function(model, recs) {
    if (recs.length > 0) {
      Ext.getCmp('detail-panel').update('<img src="' +
        recs[0].data.url + '" title="' + recs[0].data.title + '">');
      Ext.getCmp('images-view').getLayout().setActiveItem(1);
      Ext.getCmp('back-button').show();
```

```
        Ext.getCmp('rose-button').hide();
        Ext.getCmp('daffodil-button').hide();
        Ext.getCmp('hibiscus-button').hide();
    }
  }
 }
}
```

See also

▶ The recipe named *Setting up the browser-based development environment* in *Chapter 1*

▶ The recipe named *Working with Panel* in *Chapter 3*

▶ The recipe named *Designing a custom view using DataView* in this chapter

▶ The recipe named *Building wizards using CardLayout* in *Chapter 3*

5
Dealing with Data and Data Sources

In this chapter, we will cover:

- ▶ Creating models
- ▶ Loading the form using a data model
- ▶ Working with Store
- ▶ Converting incoming JSON data into models using JsonReader
- ▶ Converting incoming XML data into models using XmlReader
- ▶ Validations in models
- ▶ Defining the custom validation
- ▶ Relating models using Association
- ▶ Persisting session specific information using SessionStorageProxy
- ▶ Persisting data using LocalStorageProxy
- ▶ Accessing in-memory data using MemoryProxy
- ▶ Loading data through AJAX using AjaxProxy
- ▶ Sorting of the data
- ▶ Data grouping
- ▶ Filtering data
- ▶ Using a cross-domain URL in your application

Introduction

Imagining an application without the need for data is impossible in today's world. Almost every application has a need for data and some ways to store and work with them effectively and efficiently. Sencha Touch provides a rich set of classes to work with varied data sources, represent structured data, and store it locally, which can then be fed to different data centric components such as list, form, combo-box, charts, and so on. It also provides classes and APIs to validate, filter, sort, and group data. The following diagram depicts the different classes, which are part of the data infrastructure provided by Sencha Touch:

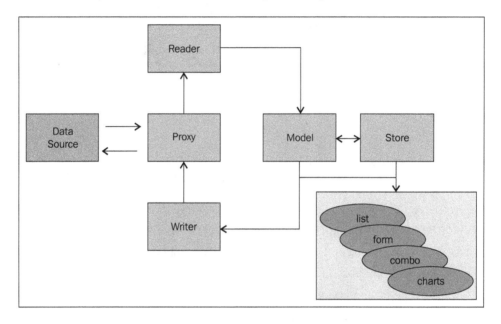

- ▸ **Proxy**: Proxies allow us to interface with different data sources such as REST services, Servlet, in-memory array, HTML5-based storage, and so on to read data from or save data to.

- ▸ **Reader**: Readers are used during the loading of the data. They interpret the data into a model or a store. Based on the type of data we have to deal with, the respective reader is used, for example, for JSON type data, `JsonReader` is used whereas for XML data, `XmlReader` is used.

- ▸ **Writer**: Writers are used during saving the data. Similar to a reader, an appropriate writer is used based on the type of data we deal with—JSON or XML.

- ▸ **Model**: Models represent the object which our application uses and works with. For example, a user, payment objects used by the application containing application specific fields and methods manipulating those fields. A store contains a collection of such models.

- ► **Store**: Stores are a collection, which contains the models, and are used by the different components. This is the class which helps us reuse the collection across multiple components. For example, the same store can be used for populating a grid, as well as in a chart.

The following diagram depicts a typical flow involving different concepts to show how the raw data from a data source is rendered in a grid:

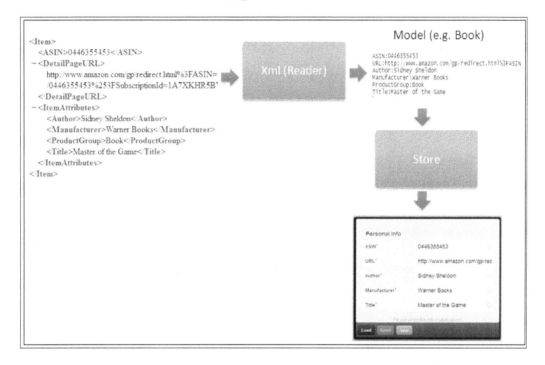

In this chapter, we will learn about every aspect of the data infrastructure provided by Sencha Touch. We will work through models to represent our data structure, use it to render views, make use of the stores and different proxies to load and save data.

Creating models

Let's start with understanding how we can represent a data structure by using a model and create objects using it.

Getting ready

Make sure that you have set up your development environment by following the recipes outlined in *Chapter 1, Gear up for the Journey.*

Create a new folder named `ch05` in the same folder where we created the `ch01` and `ch02` folders. We will be using this new folder in which to keep the code.

How to do it...

Carry out the following steps:

1. Create and open a new file named `ch05_01.js` and paste the following code into it:

```
Ext.setup({
    onReady: function() {

    Ext.regModel('User', {
        fields: [
            {name: 'name',  type: 'string'},
            {name: 'age',   type: 'int'},
            {name: 'phone', type: 'string'},
            {name: 'email', type: 'string'},
            {name: 'alive', type: 'boolean', defaultValue: true}
        ]
    });

    var user = Ext.ModelMgr.create({
        name : 'Ajit Kumar',
        age  : 24,
        phone: '555-555-5555',
        email: 'ajitkumar@walkingtree.in'
    }, 'User');

    Ext.Msg.alert('INFO', user.get('name'));
    }
});
```

2. Update the `index.html` file.
3. Deploy and access it from the browser. You may also run it using the emulator.

How it works...

Ext.regModel is a shortcut for Ext.ModelMgr.registerType using which we registered a model definition with the model manager—ModelMgr. The method does a lot of work in the background. First, it normalizes the configured associations as there are different ways that the association configuration can be specified, which we will learn more about in the *Relating models using Associations* recipe later in this chapter. After the normalization is done, it checks whether the model is extending any other model. If so, it copies all the fields, associations, and validations from the super-class model. Then, the fields and associations are created and it sets the proxy, its type, and the method that will be used to load the data into the model.

Once registered, by using the Ext.ModelMgr.create method we created a model with specific data. To the create method, we also passed the model name—User— that we had registered with the ModelMgr. Based on this, ModelMgr constructs an object for us, copies the field values, and returns it to us.

Once a model is created, ModelMgr, by default, provides getter and setter methods for every field. user.get('name') returns the value stored in the name field of the model. To set a field value, we call the setter method—user.set('age', 33).

Each field in the fields array represents Ext.data.Field. There are various useful properties supported by the field. However, in the preceding code, we have used name, type, and defaultValue properties. The type property, when specified, is used by the framework to perform the conversion and formatting of the incoming value based on the specified type. The following are the types that the Ext.data.Field supports:

- ▸ auto allows every kind of value; if no type property is specified, then auto is selected as the default
- ▸ string
- ▸ int
- ▸ float
- ▸ boolean
- ▸ date

The defaultValue property helps us to set the value that will be used as a default for a field.

For the date type field, we can also use the dateFormat property to specify the format in which the date will be converted.

Another important property on a field is convert. This accepts a function which can be used to convert the value provided by Reader into an object that will be stored in the model.

We can imagine a model as an object and due to its very nature, it also allows us to define methods inside it to implement a certain logic. Additionally, it also allows us to create a model by extending another model. Let's see how to make use of these functionalities.

Adding methods to a model

The following code snippet shows how a `changeName` method is defined inside the `User` model, which is appending an additional text to the user's name:

```
Ext.regModel('User', {
    fields: [
        {name: 'name',  type: 'string'},
        {name: 'age',   type: 'int'},
        {name: 'phone', type: 'string'},
        {name: 'email', type: 'string'},
        {name: 'alive', type: 'boolean', defaultValue: true}
    ],

    changeName: function() {
        var oldName = this.get('name'),
            newName = oldName + " Azad";

        this.set('name', newName);
    }
});
```

Once the method is defined, calling it is as easy as calling a method on any object as shown in the following code snippet:

```
user.changeName();
Ext.Msg.alert('INFO', .get('name'));//shows Ajit Kumar Azad
```

Extending a model

Sencha Touch follows object oriented approaches and methodologies. As part of this, it has also provided a mechanism to extend one class from another, though it is not something offered by JavaScript, directly. Moreover, the same has been applied to models as well, which allows us to create a model by extending an existing model. The following code snippet shows that we are defining a model named `MyUser` which is extending the `User` model and adding a new field—`dob`:

```
Ext.regModel('MyUser', {
    extend: 'User',
        fields: [
```

```
                    {name: 'dob',  type: 'string'}
        ]
    });
```

When `Ext.regModel` comes across the `extend` property, it copies all the properties of the base class—User—inside `MyUser` and hence they also become part of the new class. The following code shows instantiating `MyUser`, which ensures that the properties from the `User` class are available on `MyUser` as part of the extend mechanism:

```
var myuser = Ext.ModelMgr.create({
    name : 'Ajit Kumar',
    age  : 24,
    phone: '555-555-5555',
    email: 'ajitkumar@walkingtree.in',
    dob: '04-04-1978'
}, 'MyUser');

Ext.Msg.alert('INFO', myuser.get('name') + ' : dob : ' +
    myuser.get('dob'));
```

See also

The recipe named *Setting up the browser-based development environment* in *Chapter 1*

Loading the form using a data model

In this recipe, we will see how to make use of the model that we created in the previous recipe to populate the fields in a form.

Getting ready

Make sure that you have set up your development environment by following the recipes outlined in *Chapter 1*.

How to do it...

Carry out the following steps:

1. Create and open a new file named `ch05_02.js` and paste the following code into it:

```
Ext.setup({
    onReady: function() {

    Ext.regModel('User', {
```

```
      fields: [
        {name: 'name',  type: 'string'},
        {name: 'age',    type: 'int'},
        {name: 'phone', type: 'string'},
        {name: 'email', type: 'string'},
        {name: 'alive', type: 'boolean', defaultValue: true}
      ],

      changeName: function() {
        var oldName = this.get('name'),
        newName = oldName + " Azad";

        this.set('name', newName);
      }
});

var user = Ext.ModelMgr.create({
  name : 'Ajit Kumar',
  age  : 24,
  phone: '555-555-5555',
  email: 'ajit.kumar@walkingtree.in'
}, 'User');

user.changeName();

var form;

var formBase = {
  scroll: 'vertical',
  items: [{
    xtype: 'fieldset',
    title: 'Personal Info',
    instructions: 'Please enter the information above.',
    defaults: {
      required: true,
      labelAlign: 'left',
      labelWidth: '40%'
    },
    items: [
      {
          xtype: 'textfield',
          name : 'name',
          label: 'Name',
          useClearIcon: true,
```

```
             autoCapitalize : false
     }, {
         xtype: 'numberfield',
         name : 'age',
         label: 'Age',
         useClearIcon: false
       }, {
           xtype: 'textfield',
           name : 'phone',
           label: 'Phone',
           useClearIcon: true
         }, {
             xtype: 'emailfield',
             name : 'email',
             label: 'Email',
             placeHolder: 'you@sencha.com',
             useClearIcon: true
           }, {
             xtype: 'checkboxfield',
             name : 'alive',
             label: 'Is Alive',
             useClearIcon: true
         }]
       }
   ],
   listeners : {
       submit : function(form, result){
           console.log('success', Ext.toArray(arguments));
       },
       exception : function(form, result){
           console.log('failure', Ext.toArray(arguments));
       }
   },

   dockedItems: [
       {
           xtype: 'toolbar',
           dock: 'bottom',
           items: [
             {
               text: 'Load',
               handler: function() {
             //load fields from model
                       form.loadRecord(user);
```

```
                                }
                            },
                            {
                                text: 'Reset',
                                ui: 'decline',
                                handler: function() {
                                    form.reset();
                                }
                            },
                            {
                                text: 'Save',
                                ui: 'confirm',
                                handler: function() {
                                  Ext.Msg.alert("INFO", "In real
                                    implementation, this will be saved!");
                                }
                            }
                        }
                    ]
                }
            ]
        };

        if (Ext.is.Phone) {
          //phone specific configuration
            formBase.fullscreen = true;
        } else {
          //desktop specific configuration
            Ext.apply(formBase, {
                autoRender: true,
                floating: true,
                modal: true,
                centered: true,
                hideOnMaskTap: false,
                height: 385,
                width: 480
            });
        }

        form = new Ext.form.FormPanel(formBase);
        form.show();
        }
    });
```

2. Update the `index.html` file.

3. Deploy and access it from the browser. You may also run it using the emulator.

4. Click on the **Load** button to load model data into the fields. You will see a screen similar to the one shown in the following screenshot:

How it works...

In the preceding code, we created a model, a form panel with fields **Name**, **Age**, **Phone**, **Email**, and **Is Alive** and buttons **Load**, **Save**, **Reset** in the docked toolbar. On clicking the **Load** button, the following handler code loads the form field with the values from the `user` model:

```
form.loadRecord(user);
```

For this to work, the form field name must match with the model field name.

There's more...

When we use the model to update a view, such as a form, which has editable fields whose values can be changed by the user, a natural need arises where we question whether the model will be updated automatically. The answer is, No. If we intend to get the updated model and then work with it to, say, save then we need to do some work. Let's see what exactly we will have to do if we have to use the model to save the updated form data.

Saving form data using the associated model

The `getRecord` method of the `Ext.form.FormPanel` returns the model instance currently loaded into the `form`. However, the model is not automatically updated when the field value changes. If we want to get an updated model at any instance of time, then the following piece of code should be written inside the **Save** button handler:

```
var formValues = form.getValues();
user.set(formValues); //updates the values and marks
  the instance dirty
user.save();  //saves the data
```

Once we have updated our model, the `save` method takes care of saving it to the appropriate data source. The detail about how it identifies which data source and how it knows whether the data needs to be sent in XML or JSON format, and so on, will be covered in the subsequent recipes.

See also

▶ The recipe named *Setting up the browser-based development environment* in *Chapter 1*

▶ The recipe named *Getting your form ready with FormPanel* in *Chapter 2*

▶ The recipe named *Working with the select field* in *Chapter 2*

▶ The recipe named *Creating models* in this chapter

Working with Store

So far, we saw how to define and create a model and use it to populate a form. There are various other components which work with a collection of models that need to be saved in a store. In this recipe, we will look at the steps required to define a store and use it to contain models and populate the data in a component.

Getting ready

Make sure that you have set up your development environment by following the recipes outlined in *Chapter 1*.

How to do it...

Carry out the following steps:

1. Create and open a new file named `ch05_03.js` and paste the following code into it:

```
Ext.setup({
    onReady: function() {

    Ext.regModel('User', {
        fields: [
            {name: 'name',  type: 'string'},
            {name: 'age',    type: 'int'},
            {name: 'phone', type: 'string'},
            {name: 'email', type: 'string'},
            {name: 'alive', type: 'boolean', defaultValue: true}
        ]
    });

    var store = new Ext.data.Store({
        model: 'User',
        data : [{
        name : 'Ajit Kumar',
        age  : 32,
        phone: '555-555-5555',
        email: 'ajit@walkingtree.in'
    }, {
        name : 'Alok Ranjan',
        age  : 32,
        phone: '123-456-7890',
        email: 'alok@walkingtree.in'
    }, {
        name : 'Pradeep Lavania',
        age  : 34,
        phone: '987-654-3210',
        email: 'pradeep@walkingtree.in'
    }
        ]
    });
```

```
            var form;

            var formBase = {
                scroll: 'vertical',
                items: [{
                        xtype: 'selectfield',
                        name : 'user',
                        label: 'User',
                        store: store,
                        valueField: 'name',
                        displayField: 'name'
                    }]
            };

            if (Ext.is.Phone) {
                formBase.fullscreen = true;
            } else {
                Ext.apply(formBase, {
                    autoRender: true,
                    floating: true,
                    modal: true,
                    centered: true,
                    hideOnMaskTap: false,
                    height: 385,
                    width: 480
                });
            }

            form = new Ext.form.FormPanel(formBase);
            form.show();
            }
    });
```

2. Update the `index.html` file.

3. Deploy and access it from the browser. You may also run it using the emulator. You will see a screen similar to the one shown in the following screenshot:

How it works...

In the preceding code, we create a form panel with a combobox with a store associated with it. The following code creates a `store` object using the inline data containing the user information:

```
var store = new Ext.data.Store({
    model: 'User',
    data : [{
    name : 'Ajit Kumar',
    age  : 32,
    phone: '555-555-5555',
    email: 'ajit@walkingtree.in'
}, {
    name : 'Alok Ranjan',
    age  : 32,
    phone: '123-456-7890',
    email: 'alok@walkingtree.in'
}, {
    name : 'Pradeep Lavania',
```

```
        age   : 34,
        phone: '987-654-3210',
        email: 'pradeep@walkingtree.in'
    }
  ]
});
```

The `model` property on `store` instructs the `store` that each item in the `data` array will be converted into a `User` model. After this, we created a combobox using the store in the following code:

```
items: [{
    xtype: 'selectfield',
    name : 'user',
    label: 'User',
    store: store,
    valueField: 'name',
    displayField: 'name'
}]
```

`valueField` and `displayField` contain the model field names whose value will be read to populate the combobox. In our code, both fields are using the `name` field, so we see the user name appearing in the selection list.

There's more...

In the recipe, we saw how to make use of the inline data to populate a store and subsequently the combobox. In an application, we may have a need to add the records dynamically to the store based on certain application logic. Let's see how we can do it.

Adding records to a store at runtime

There are multiple options depending upon what exactly we want to do. Let's visit each of the options and understand what the specific usage of them is.

The following code shows appending an array of JSON objects to the store using the `loadData` method:

```
store.loadData([{
    name : 'Priti',
    age  : 30,
    phone: '987-654-3210',
    email: 'priti@walkingtree.in'
}], true);
```

The second parameter indicates whether the new data needs to be appended if it is set to `true`. If we pass `false`, then the old data from the store is cleared and the new data is added to it.

The same functionality can be achieved by calling the `add` method, which appends the new data to the end of the existing record set as follows:

```
store.add({
    name : 'Priti',
    age  : 30,
    phone: '987-654-3210',
    email: 'priti@walkingtree.in'
});
```

If we want to insert the new record at a specific position in `store`, then the `insert` method can be used, as shown in the following code snippet, where we are adding the new record at index 1:

```
store.insert(1, {
    name : 'Priti',
    age  : 30,
    phone: '987-654-3210',
    email: 'priti@walkingtree.in'
});
```

Last but not least, if we have models and want to use them to add records to `store`, we use the `loadRecords` method on `store` as follows:

```
var user = Ext.ModelMgr.create({
    name : 'Pratyush Kumar',
    age  : 5,
    phone: '987-654-3210'
}, 'User');

    store.loadRecords([user], true);
```

See also

 ► The recipe named *Setting up the browser-based development environment* in *Chapter 1*
 ► The recipe named *Getting your form ready with FormPanel* in *Chapter 2*
 ► The recipe named *Working with the select field* in *Chapter 2*
 ► The recipe named *Creating models* in this chapter

Converting incoming JSON data into models using JsonReader

As we saw earlier in the chapter, a reader helps us in data loading and converting the incoming data into a model, which can then be added to a store. Based on the type of data, Sencha Touch provides two readers – JsonReader and XmlReader. In this recipe we will see how to make use of the JsonReader to read the JSON data and prepare a model out of it.

Getting ready

Make sure that you have set up your development environment by following the recipes outlined in *Chapter 1*.

How to do it...

Carry out the following steps:

1. Create and open a new file named users.json and paste the following into it:

```json
{"users": [{
    "id": "1",
     "name" : "Ajit Kumar",
     "age"   : "32",
     "phone": "555-555-5555",
     "email": "ajit@walkingtree.in"
}, {
    "id": "2",
     "name" : "Alok Ranjan",
     "age"   : "32",
     "phone": "123-456-7890",
     "email": "alok@walkingtree.in"
}, {
    "id": "3",
     "name" : "Pradeep Lavania",
     "age"   : "34",
     "phone": "987-654-3210",
     "email": "pradeep@walkingtree.in"
}]
```

2. Create and open a new file named `ch05_04.js` and paste the following code into it:

```
Ext.setup({
    onReady: function() {

  Ext.regModel('User', {
      fields: [
        'id',
          {name: 'name',  type: 'string'},
          {name: 'age',   type: 'int'},
          {name: 'phone', type: 'string'},
          {name: 'email', type: 'string'},
          {name: 'alive', type: 'boolean', defaultValue: true}
      ]
  });

  var store = new Ext.data.Store({
      model: 'User',
      autoLoad: true,
      proxy: {
        type: 'ajax',
        url : 'users.json',
        reader: {
            type: 'json',
            root: 'users'
        }
      }
  });

    var form;

    var formBase = {
        scroll: 'vertical',
        items: [{
                  xtype: 'selectfield',
                  name : 'user',
                  label: 'User',
                  store: store,
                  valueField: 'name',
                  displayField: 'name'
                }]
    };

    if (Ext.is.Phone) {
        formBase.fullscreen = true;
```

```
        } else {
            Ext.apply(formBase, {
                autoRender: true,
                floating: true,
                modal: true,
                centered: true,
                hideOnMaskTap: false,
                height: 385,
                width: 480
            });
        }

        form = new Ext.form.FormPanel(formBase);
        form.show();
        }
    });
```

3. Update the `index.html` file.

4. Deploy and access it from the browser. You may also run it using the emulator.

How it works...

The code creates a form panel with a selection field which shows the list of users loaded by `store` from the `users.json` file. The `users.json` file contains the user information in the JSON encoded form.

The following code creates a store by using an Ajax proxy and `url` pointing to the `users.json` file:

```
var store = new Ext.data.Store({
    model: 'User',
    autoLoad: true,
    proxy: {
        type: 'ajax',
        url : 'users.json',
        reader: {
            type: 'json',
            root: 'users'
        }
    }
});
```

The proxy uses the JSON reader, which is indicated by the `type` property of `reader`. The other important property on the reader is `root` which needs to be set to the property in the `users.json` file which contains the data array. Hence, it is set to `users`.

Once the `proxy` and `reader` is setup on the `store`, the store knows from where it has to load the data (proxy detail) and how the data needs to be interpreted (reader detail) to construct the model. One thing left is when to load the date? For this, we set the `autoLoad` property on `store` to `true`. This will instruct the store to start loading the data as soon as it is initialized.

More about the proxy and reader is covered in the recipes to follow.

There's more...

There are different properties provided by the proxy and reader to help us deal with different incoming data structures. In the next section, we will see how to deal with some of the data structures such as nested data and metadata.

Fetching a record from a nested data

Say, if our data contains some metadata about each data such that the actual record is nested as shown in the following data format:

```
{"users": [{
    "id": "1234",
    "count": "1",
    "user" : {
    "id": "1",
      "name" : "Ajit Kumar",
      "age"   : "32",
      "phone": "555-555-5555",
      "email": "ajit@walkingtree.in"
    }
  }, {
    "id": "1234",
    "count": "1",
    "user" : {
    "id": "2",
      "name" : "Alok Ranjan",
      "age"   : "32",
      "phone": "123-456-7890",
      "email": "alok@walkingtree.in"
    }
  }, {
    "id": "1234",
    "count": "1",
    "user" : {
    "id": "3",
      "name" : "Pradeep Lavania",
```

```
            "age"  : "34",
            "phone": "987-654-3210",
            "email": "pradeep@walkingtree.in"
        }
    }]
}
```

To fetch the actual user information from the above structure, we will have to make use of the `record` property on `reader` to indicate the nested field that contains the user information as follows:

```
reader: {
    type: 'json',
    root: 'users',
    record: 'user'
}
```

Working with response metadata

Sometimes, the response contains the metadata and the actual data. These metadata contain application specific information, which can be used by the client-side code to exhibit certain behaviors. For example, one of the important pieces of information which helps our application to implement pagination is the total record count returned along with the page data, so that the frontend would be able to derive the number of pages of data it will have to deal with and, accordingly, render the page information or handle the previous/next functionality. Similarly, the server-side application may have to indicate whether the request was processed successfully or if there was an error. This may be achieved by the server side by returning a property in the metadata and setting it to true/false to indicate success/error. The following code shows the record structure where `totalRecords` and `success` are two metadata properties being returned from the server besides the actual data—`users`:

```
{
  "totalRecords" : "20",
  "success" : "true",
  "users": [{
    "id": "1",
      "name" : "Ajit Kumar",
      "age"  : "32",
  ........
  }]
}
```

There are two additional properties provided by the reader: `totalProperty` and `successProperty` to map the field on the server response which contains the total number of records available with the server (although it is returning only three in a read) and the field that would indicate whether there was any application level error while processing the request. For example, if the application failed to get users from its database, it can make use of the success field to convey the error to the frontend. The following code shows the changes that we will have to make to the reader to accommodate these two additional metadata properties:

```
reader: {
    type: 'json',
    root: 'users',
    totalProperty: 'totalRecords',
    successProperty: 'success'
}
```

See also

- ▶ The recipe named *Setting up the browser-based development environment* in *Chapter 1*

- ▶ The recipe named *Getting your form ready with FormPanel* in *Chapter 2*

- ▶ The recipe named *Working with the select field* in *Chapter 2*

- ▶ The recipe named *Creating models* in this chapter

- ▶ The recipe named *Working with Store* in this chapter

- ▶ The recipe named *Loading data through AJAX using AjaxProxy* in this chapter

Converting incoming XML data into models using XmlReader

Similar to the `JsonReader`, `XmlReader` exists for us to work with the XML data efficiently. It provides XPath kind of notation to quickly access the elements of the incoming XML data.

In this recipe, we will see how to work with the XML data and use `XmlReader` to construct the model, which can be used within the application.

Getting ready

Make sure that you have set up your development environment by following the recipes outlined in *Chapter 1*.

How to do it...

Carry out the following steps:

1. Create and open a new file named `users.xml` and paste the following code into it:

```xml
<?xml version="1.0" encoding="UTF-8"?>
<users>
    <id>1</id>
    <name>Ajit Kumar</name>
    <age>33</age>
    <phone>123-456-7890</phone>
    <email>ajit.kumar@walingtree.in</email>
    <alive>true</alive>
</user>
<user>
    <id>2</id>
    <name>Alok Ranjan</name>
    <age>34</age>
    <phone>123-456-7890</phone>
    <email>alok@walkingtree.in</email>
    <alive>true</alive>
</user>
</users>
```

2. Create and open a new file named `ch05_05.js` and paste the following code into it:

```javascript
Ext.setup({
    onReady: function() {

    Ext.regModel('User', {
        fields: [
            {name: 'name',  type: 'string'},
            {name: 'age',   type: 'int'},
            {name: 'phone', type: 'string'},
            {name: 'email', type: 'string'},
            {name: 'alive', type: 'boolean', defaultValue: true}
        ]
    });

    var store = new Ext.data.Store({
        model: 'User',
        autoLoad: true,
        proxy: {
            type: 'ajax',
```

```
        url : 'users.xml',
        reader: {
          type: 'xml',
          record: 'user'
        }
      }
    });

    var form;

    var formBase = {
      scroll: 'vertical',
      items: [{
        xtype: 'selectfield',
        name : 'user',
        label: 'User',
        store: store,
        valueField: 'name',
        displayField: 'name'
      }]
    };

    if (Ext.is.Phone) {
      formBase.fullscreen = true;
    } else {
        Ext.apply(formBase, {
          autoRender: true,
          floating: true,
          modal: true,
          centered: true,
          hideOnMaskTap: false,
          height: 385,
          width: 480
        });
      }

      form = new Ext.form.FormPanel(formBase);
      form.show();
    }
  });
```

3. Update the `index.html` file.
4. Deploy and access it from the browser. You may also run it using the emulator.

How it works...

The code loads the data from the `users.xml` file and populates the items in the selection field of the form panel. The `store` is modified to use `proxy` with `url` set to the `users.xml` file and `reader` is configured on the proxy with `type xml`, so that it can interpret the incoming XML data into the model.

```
var store = new Ext.data.Store({
    model: 'User',
    autoLoad: true,
    proxy: {
      type: 'ajax',
      url : 'users.xml',
      reader: {
          type: 'xml',
          record: 'user'
      }
    }
});
```

For XML reader, we have used the property `record` to tell which element in the incoming XML represents the user information.

See also

- ▶ The recipe named *Setting up the browser-based development environment* in *Chapter 1*
- ▶ The recipe named *Getting your form ready with FormPanel* in *Chapter 2*
- ▶ The recipe named *Working with Select field* in *Chapter 2*
- ▶ The recipe named *Working with Store* in this chapter
- ▶ The recipe named *Loading data through AJAX using AjaxProxy* in this chapter

Validations in models

A model definition represents the structure of the data which has one or more fields, for example, a `Payment` model containing a `paymentDate` field to store the date when the payment was made. Now, when we construct models using the incoming data, there may be certain rules that we would like to apply to make sure that the model represents valid data. For example, on a `Payment` model, it may be required to have a `paymentDate` field and also it may be required that the value in this field is in the past (prior to today's date). This kind of mechanism helps us to build robust applications.

Sencha Touch provides support for this by using `validations` on `Model`. There are pre-defined lists of validations, which we can use to setup the validation rules on our model. The following are the pre-defined validations supported:

- `presence`: Validates that a given property is present
- `length`: Validates if the given value is between the specified min and max
- `inclusion`: Validates that the value is present in the specified list
- `exclusion`: Validates that the value is not present in the specified list
- `format`: Validates that the value matches with the specified regular expression

In this recipe, we will see how to make use of these validations.

Getting ready

Make sure that you have set up your development environment by following the recipes outlined in *Chapter 1*.

How to do it...

Carry out the following steps:

1. Create and open a new file named `ch05_06.js` and paste the following code into it:

```
Ext.setup({
    onReady: function() {

    Ext.regModel('User', {
        fields: [
            {name: 'name',  type: 'string'},
            {name: 'age',   type: 'int'},
            {name: 'phone', type: 'string'},
            {name: 'email', type: 'string'},
            {name: 'alive', type: 'boolean', defaultValue: true}
        ],
        validations: [
            {type: 'presence',  field: 'age'},
            {type: 'length',    field: 'name',    min: 2}
        ]
    });

    var user = Ext.ModelMgr.create({
        name : '',
        phone: '555-555-5555',
        email: 'ajit.kumar@walkingtree.in'
```

```
      }, 'User');

    var errors = user.validate();
    if (!errors.isValid()) {
      var errStr = '';
      Ext.each(errors.items, function(error, index, allErrors){
        errStr += error.field + ' : ' + error.message + '\n';
      });
      alert(errStr);
    }
    }
  });
```

2. Update the `index.html` file.

3. Deploy and access it from the browser. You may also run it using the emulator.

How it works...

The preceding code sets up the validation rules on the model and validates the model objects using them.

```
validations: [
          {type: 'presence',   field: 'age'},
          {type: 'length',     field: 'name',     min: 2}
      ]
```

By using the preceding code, we configured two validation rules: `presence` and `length` on the `age` and `name` fields, respectively. The rules suggest that we want to make sure that a model must have the `age` field in it and the `name` must be at least two characters long.

```
    var errors = user.validate();
```

The preceding line validates the `user` model where it applies all the validations that we had configured on the `User` model. The `validate` method returns `Ext.data.Errors` as the error object. `errors.isValid()` returns `true` if the model has passed the validations.

```
    if (!errors.isValid()) {
      var errStr = '';
      Ext.each(errors.items, function(error, index, allErrors){
        errStr += error.field + ' : ' + error.message + '\n';
      });
      alert(errStr);
    }
```

In case of an error, the `validate` method returns an array of error items. Each will have a `field` indicating the model field that has failed the validation and the corresponding `message`. In the preceding code, we iterated through the `errors.items` array, concatenated all the error fields and their messages, and displayed them as shown in the following screenshot:

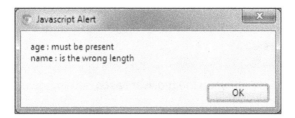

There's more...

In the following sections, we will see how to make use of the other validations.

Inclusion

Inclusion works with the `list` property which contains an array of strings. The validation logic for `inclusion` checks if the value is present in the specified list.

The following line shows the typical usage of the `inclusion` validation:

```
{type: 'inclusion',    field: 'gender',    list: ['Male', 'Female']}
```

Exclusion

Exclusion works as a complement of `inclusion`, where it returns `true` (validation passed) if the value does not belong to the specified list. Usage is exactly the same as `inclusion`, except that the type will be `'exclusion'`.

Format

Format helps us to verify if the value matches with the specified regular expression. We can use the JavaScript regular expressions to create any matchers. This validation rule works on the `matcher` property. The following is a sample usage:

```
{type: 'format',field: 'username', matcher: /([a-z]+)[0-9]{2,3}/}
```

Changing the default message

By default, the `Ext.data.validations` class defines the messages for each type of validation rules. For example, if the `presence` validation fails, then **must be present** appears for the field for which it had failed. If the default message is not the desired one, then we can change it by specifying the `message` property for the validation as follows:

```
{type: 'presence',  message: ' property not found', field: 'age'}
```

See also

▶ The recipe named *Setting up the browser-based development environment* in *Chapter 1*

▶ The recipe named *Creating models* in this chapter

▶ The recipe named *Validating your form* in *Chapter 2*

Defining the custom validation

In the previous recipe, we saw out-of-the-box validations available in Sencha Touch. However, for various practical reasons, we may have a need to create additional validation rules and use them across the application. For example, the payment amount must not be negative; date must be prior to today's date, and so on.

In this recipe, we will go through the steps to create a new validation rule and use it in the application.

Getting ready

Make sure that you have set up your development environment by following the recipes outlined in *Chapter 1*.

How to do it...

Carry out the following steps:

1. Create and open a new file named `ch05_07.js` and paste the following code into it:

```
Ext.setup({
    onReady: function() {

    Ext.apply(Ext.data.validations, {

        checkdateMessage: 'date is not within the allowed range',
```

```
  checkdate: function(config, value) {
    if (value === undefined) {
      return false;
    }

    var graceDays = Ext.isEmpty(config.grace) ? 1 :
      config.grace;

    var date = Date.parseDate(value, 'd-m-Y');
    var currDate = new Date();
    currDate.clearTime();
    if (date.between(currDate, currDate.add(Date.DAY,
        graceDays)))
      return true;
    else
      return false;

  }
});

 Ext.regModel('User', {
    fields: [
        {name: 'name',  type: 'string'},
        {name: 'age',    type: 'int'},
        {name: 'phone', type: 'string'},
        {name: 'email', type: 'string'},
        {name: 'effectiveDate', type: 'string'},  //format d-m-Y
        {name: 'alive', type: 'boolean', defaultValue: true}
    ],
    validations: [
        {type: 'presence',  field: 'age'},
        {type: 'length',    field: 'name',    min: 2},
        {type: 'checkdate', field: 'effectiveDate',   grace: 2}
    ]
});

var user = Ext.ModelMgr.create({
    name : '',
    phone: '555-555-5555',
    email: 'ajit.kumar@walkingtree.in',
    effectiveDate: '23-07-2011'
}, 'User');

var errors = user.validate();
```

```
       if (!errors.isValid()) {
         var errStr = '';
         Ext.each(errors.items, function(error, index, allErrors){
           errStr += error.field + ' : ' + error.message + '\n';
         });
         alert(errStr);
       }
     }
  });
```

2. Update the `index.html` file.

3. Deploy and access it from the browser. You may also run it using the emulator.

How it works...

```
     Ext.apply(Ext.data.validations, {
```

`Ext.data.validations` contains all the five validation rules and is a singleton class. Using `Ext.apply`, we are adding additional validation to it:

```
     checkdateMessage: 'date is not within the allowed range',
```

`checkdateMessage`, once defined, will be used by the `validate` method to show the message in the errors when a field with the new validation—`checkdate`—fails. The syntax for this property is `<name of the validation rule>Message`. So, for our new validation rule `checkdate`, this has been named as `checkdateMessage`.

```
     checkdate: function(config, value) {
       if (value === undefined) {
         return false;
       }

       var graceDays = Ext.isEmpty(config.grace) ? 1 : config.grace;

       var date = Date.parseDate(value, 'd-m-Y');
       var currDate = new Date();
       currDate.clearTime();
       if (date.between(currDate, currDate.add(Date.DAY, graceDays)))
         return true;
       else
         return false;

     }
```

The preceding code defines the core logic of the new validation rule `checkdate`. All it is doing is returning `true` if the passed date value is within the specified `grace` days from today. If the function returns `true`, it means the validation has passed. If `false` is returned, then the framework adds the field name and the corresponding message to the errors array.

Once the new validation rule is defined, we added it to the validations:

```
{type: 'checkdate', field: 'effectiveDate',   grace: 2}
```

where we mentioned that `effectiveDate` must be between today and today+2 days, and then we passed the `effectiveDate` on the model:

```
effectiveDate: '23-07-2011'
```

When the validation fails, the following errors show up:

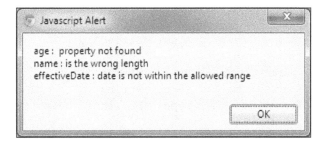

See also

- ▶ The recipe named *Setting up the browser-based development environment* in *Chapter 1*
- ▶ The recipe named *Creating models* in this chapter
- ▶ The recipe named *Validations in models* in this chapter

Relating models using association

In an application, we generally deal with multiple types of models, for example, user, address, order, payment, account, and so on. Some models are self-sufficient. However, there will be some models that are related to each other, and there is an association which exists between them. For example, a user can have one or more addresses, a user may place one or more orders, and an order may have one or more payments made against it, and so on. In a typical relational database, we have entities and the relationship between them. The same can be achieved with models using the association mechanism provided by Sencha Touch. This recipe will demonstrate how to define associations between models, which are used by the reader, internally, to populate nested models for us.

Getting ready

Make sure that you have set up your development environment by following the recipes outlined in *Chapter 1*.

How to do it...

Carry out the following steps:

1. Create and open a new file named `ch05_08.js` and paste the following code into it:

```
Ext.setup({
    onReady: function() {

    Ext.regModel('User', {
        fields: [
            {name: 'name',  type: 'string'},
            {name: 'age',   type: 'int'},
            {name: 'phone', type: 'string'},
            {name: 'email', type: 'string'},
            {name: 'alive', type: 'boolean', defaultValue: true}

        ],
        hasMany: {model: 'Address', name: 'addresses'}
    });

    Ext.regModel('Address', {
     fields: ['id', 'line1', 'line2', 'zipcode', 'state', 'country']
    });


    var user = Ext.ModelMgr.create({
      name : 'Ajit Kumar',
      age  : 24,
      phone: '555-555-5555',
      email: 'ajit.kumar@walkingtree.in',
      addresses: [{
        id: 1,
        line1: 'Flat# 101, Plot# 101, Elegance Apartment',
        line2: 'New SBH Colony, East Maredpally, Hyderabad',
        zipcode: '500023',
        state: 'AP',
        country: 'India'
      }, {
```

```
            id: 2,
            line1: 'Janapriya Utopia',
            line2: 'Hyderguda, Hyderabad',
            zipcode: '500081',
            state: 'AP',
            country: 'India'
        }]
    }, 'User');

    alert('Number of addresses: ' + user.get('addresses').length);
    }

});
```

2. Update the `index.html` file.
3. Deploy and access it from the browser. You may also run it using the emulator.

How it works...

In the preceding code, we defined two models: `User` and `Address` and established the `hasMany` association between them such that a user can have multiple addresses. The `hasMany` association helps us establish a one-to-many relationship:

```
hasMany: {model: 'Address', name: 'addresses'}
```

The preceding line in the `User` model definition indicates that the `User` model has `hasMany` association with the `Address` model where the `addresses` is a reference with which we can access the addresses associated with a particular user.

Then, we added `addresses` to the user while creating an instance of the `User` model:

```
var user = Ext.ModelMgr.create({
    name : 'Ajit Kumar',
    age  : 24,
    phone: '555-555-5555',
    email: 'ajit.kumar@walkingtree.in',
    addresses: [{
      id: 1,
      line1: 'Flat# 101, Plot# 101, Elegance Apartment',
      line2: 'New SBH Colony, East Maredpally, Hyderabad',
      zipcode: '500023',
      state: 'AP',
      country: 'India'
    }, {
      id: 2,
```

```
        line1: 'Janapriya Utopia',
        line2: 'Hyderguda, Hyderabad',
        zipcode: '500081',
        state: 'AP',
        country: 'India'
    }]
  }, 'User');
```

`user.get('addresses')` returns the array of addresses associated with the `user` model as the model manager automatically provides the `getter` and `setter` methods for every model field.

There's more...

Like `hasMany`, Sencha Touch provides another association mechanism named `belongsTo`. Let's see what it is and where we can use it.

Many-to-one association

`belongsTo` is used to establish many-to-one association. This is a way to access the parent/owner model from the child. For example, a user can have multiple addresses. For a user, if we have to get the addresses, we can do this by putting a `hasMany` association between the `User` and the `Address` in the `User` model. However, if for an address, we want to get the corresponding `User`, then we can define the `belongsTo` association in the `Address` model with the `User` model. A point to remember in this association is that we must establish a foreign key relationship with the parent/owner model. The following code shows the modified `Address` model with the `belongsTo` association:

```
Ext.regModel('Address', {
  fields: ['id', 'line1', 'line2', 'zipcode', 'state', 'country',
    'user_id']
  ,belongsTo: 'User'
});
```

Moreover, when we instantiate the address, we will specify the `user_id`, as follows:

```
{
    id: 1,
    user_id: 1,
    line1: 'Flat# 101, Plot# 101, Elegance Apartment',
    line2: 'New SBH Colony, East Maredpally, Hyderabad',
    zipcode: '500023',
    state: 'AP',
    country: 'India'
}
```

The framework is intelligent enough to generate the `getter` and `setter` methods for us based on the association. On the `address` model, we can use `getUser()` and `setUser()` methods to work with the model, and based on the proxy setup on the model, it will load/save the `user` model for us.

See also

▶ The recipe named *Setting up the browser-based development environment* in *Chapter 1*

▶ The recipe named *Creating models* in this chapter

Persisting session-specific data using SessionStorageProxy

So far in this chapter we have learned how to create a model, store it as a collection in a store, establish relationships and carry out the validations. However, all this was happening in memory. One page refresh and all our models will be re-initialized and stores re-constructed. It would be a lot better if we could persist them and use them for a longer interval. Persistence capability is provided to us by `Proxy`. Now let's see how to work with the specific proxies to load and save models. The following are types of proxies supported by Sencha Touch:

▶ `ClientProxy`: Helps us to persist a model on the client browser and load it from that storage

▶ `MemoryProxy`: Uses an in-memory storage

▶ `SessionStorageProxy`: Uses HTML5 session storage

▶ `LocalStorageProxy`: Uses HTML5 local storage

▶ `ServerProxy`: Helps us to persist a model on the server and load it from the remote server

▶ `AjaxProxy`: Used with the server in the same domain where the application is being accessed

▶ `ScriptTagProxy`: Used to connect to a server which is deployed in a domain different from the application domain

In this recipe, we will see how to make use of `SessionStorageProxy` to persist the model and restore it from the storage.

Getting ready

Make sure that you have set up your development environment by following the recipes outlined in *Chapter 1*.

How to do it...

Carry out the following steps:

1. Create and open a new file named `ch05_09.js` and paste the following code into it:

```
Ext.setup({
    onReady: function() {

    Ext.regModel('User', {
        fields: [
            {name: 'id',    type: 'int'},
            {name: 'name',  type: 'string'},
            {name: 'age',   type: 'int'},
            {name: 'phone', type: 'string'},
            {name: 'email', type: 'string'},
            {name: 'alive', type: 'boolean', defaultValue: true}

        ],
        hasMany: {model: 'Address', name: 'addresses'},
        proxy: {
            type: 'sessionstorage',
            id : '5443ch05sessionkey'
        }
    });

    Ext.regModel('Address', {
        fields: ['id', 'line1', 'line2', 'zipcode', 'state',
          'country'],

        belongsTo: 'User'
    });


    var user = Ext.ModelMgr.create({
    id: 1,
      name : 'Ajit Kumar',
      age  : 24,
      phone: '555-555-5555',
```

```
      email: 'ajit.kumar@walkingtree.in',
      addresses: [{
        id: 1,
        line1: 'Flat# 101, Plot# 101, Elegance Apartment',
        line2: 'New SBH Colony, East Maredpally, Hyderabad',
        zipcode: '500023',
        state: 'AP',
        country: 'India'
      }, {
        id: 2,
        line1: 'Janapriya Utopia',
        line2: 'Hyderguda, Hyderabad',
        zipcode: '500081',
        state: 'AP',
        country: 'India'
      }]
    }, 'User');

//save the model
  user.save({
    success: function() {
        console.log('The User was saved');
    }});

//load model from the storage
    User = Ext.ModelMgr.getModel('User');
    User.load(1, {
    success: function(record, operation) {
        console.log('The User was loaded');
        alert('Name: ' + record.get('name') + ' : Addresses : ' +
          record.get('addresses').length);
    }});
  }

});
```

2. Update the `index.html` file.

3.   Deploy and access it from the browser. You may also run it using the emulator. You
     will see the following content in the **Session Storage** of Google Chrome:

How it works...

In the preceding code, we set up `proxy` on the model and configured `sessionstorage`
as the `proxy type`, which allows us to persist data in the browser provided HTML5-based
`Sessionstorage`. `id` is an important property and the value in it must be unique within the
session. If the IDs are not unique, we will run the risk of one part of the application overwriting
the data, which was stored by some other part of the application.

```
proxy: {
        type: 'sessionstorage',
        id : '5443ch05sessionkey'
}
```

After `proxy` is set up on the model, it is persisted by calling the `save` method as follows:

```
user.save({
  success: function() {
      console.log('The User was saved');
  }});
```

Then, we are loading the persisted model from the session storage where the user ID is 1:

```
User.load(1, {
  success: function(record, operation) {
    console.log('The User was loaded');
    alert('Name: ' + record.get('name') + ' : Addresses : ' +
      record.get('addresses').length);
  }});
```

On successful load of the model from the session storage, the callback registered for
`success` is called.

If this proxy is used in a browser where session storage is not supported, the constructor will throw an error.

There's more...

The code that we saw in the recipe uses the model and the associated proxy to save it in the storage. However, alternatively, we can also use the store to save models contained by the `store`. In the following section, we will see how to make use of the store to do so.

Working through the store

To go through the store, replace:

```
//save the model
  user.save({
    success: function() {
        console.log('The User was saved');
    }});
```

with the following:

```
store.add(user);
store.sync();
```

This will ensure that the user model is saved in the storage.

Similarly, to read the data from the storage, we can use `store.load()` to read all the stored models.

See also

- ▶ The recipe named *Setting up the browser-based development environment* in *Chapter 1*
- ▶ The recipe named *Creating models* in this chapter

Persisting data using LocalStorageProxy

This recipe describes the usage of HTML5 provided local storage. This persists the data across sessions.

Getting ready

Make sure that you have set up your development environment by following the recipes outlined in *Chapter 1*.

How to do it...

```
proxy: {
        type: 'localstorage',
        id : '5443ch05localkey'
    }
```

How it works...

The preceding code uses the local storage proxy to store the data on the browser. Similar to `SessionStorageProxy`, this also requires a unique ID against which the data is stored and used to retrieve.

See also

▶ The recipe named *Setting up the browser-based development environment* in Chapter 1

▶ The recipe named *Creating models* in this chapter

▶ The recipe named *Persisting session specific information using SessionStorageProxy* in this chapter

Accessing in-memory data using MemoryProxy

The simplest form, yet very temporary, is to save and load data in an in-memory variable. In the *Working with Store* recipe, we used the inline data to load records in the store. However, that does not utilize the reader. In order to use the capabilities of the reader, we have to use `proxy`. MemoryProxy is an implementation of the `proxy` class to help us work with the in-memory data and use the reader's capabilities. This recipe shows how to use the memory proxy.

Getting ready

Make sure that you have set up your development environment by following the recipes outlined in *Chapter 1*.

How to do it...

Carry out the following steps:

1. Create and open a new file named ch05_11.js and paste the following code into it:

```
Ext.setup({
    onReady: function() {
    Ext.regModel('User', {
        fields: [
            {name: 'name',  type: 'string'},
            {name: 'age',   type: 'int'},
            {name: 'phone', type: 'string'},
            {name: 'email', type: 'string'},
            {name: 'alive', type: 'boolean', defaultValue: true}
        ]
    });
    var data = {users: [{
        id: 1,
          name : 'Ajit Kumar',
          age  : 32,
          phone: '555-555-5555',
          email: 'ajit@walkingtree.in'
      }, {
        id: 2,
          name : 'Alok Ranjan',
          age  : 32,
          phone: '123-456-7890',
          email: 'alok@walkingtree.in'
      }, {
        id: 3,
          name : 'Pradeep Lavania',
          age  : 34,
          phone: '987-654-3210',
          email: 'pradeep@walkingtree.in'
      }]
    };
    var store = new Ext.data.Store({
        model: 'User',
        autoLoad: true,
        data: data,
        proxy: {
```

```
                type: 'memory',
                reader: {
                    type: 'json',
                    root: 'users'
                }
            }
        });

        var form;

        var formBase = {
            scroll: 'vertical',
            items: [{
                    xtype: 'selectfield',
                    name : 'user',
                    label: 'User',
                    store: store,
                    valueField: 'name',
                    displayField: 'name'
                }]
        };

        if (Ext.is.Phone) {
            formBase.fullscreen = true;
        } else {
            Ext.apply(formBase, {
                autoRender: true,
                floating: true,
                modal: true,
                centered: true,
                hideOnMaskTap: false,
                height: 385,
                width: 480
            });
        }

        form = new Ext.form.FormPanel(formBase);
        form.show();
        }
    });
```

2. Update the `index.html` file.

3. Deploy and access it from the browser. You may also run it using the emulator.

How it works...

```
var store = new Ext.data.Store({
    model: 'User',
    autoLoad: true,
    data: data,
    proxy: {
      type: 'memory',
      reader: {
          type: 'json',
          root: 'users'
      }
    }
});
```

Setting `type` to `memory` sets up the `MemoryProxy` on the store. Memory proxy works only on the in-memory data, which we have stored in the `data` variable. As `data` represents a JSON format of the data; we configured the `json` type `reader` and used the `root` to point to the property in the data which contains the actual user information.

See also

▶ The recipe named *Setting up the browser-based development environment* in *Chapter 1*

▶ The recipe named *Getting your form ready with FormPanel* in *Chapter 2*

▶ The recipe named *Working with the select field* in *Chapter 2*

▶ The recipe named *Working with Store* in this chapter

Loading data through AJAX using AjaxProxy

In the last three recipes, we saw the usage of the different types of client-side proxies, which help us persist the data on the client browser. Now, we will see how to work with the server proxies to persist the data on a remote server.

In this recipe, we will see what it takes to use `AjaxProxy` to persist and load models.

Getting ready

Make sure that you have set up your development environment by following the recipes outlined in *Chapter 1*.

How to do it...

Carry out the following steps:

1. Create and open a new file named `ch05_12.js` and paste the following code into it:

```
Ext.setup({
    onReady: function() {
  Ext.regModel('User', {
      fields: [
            {name: 'name',  type: 'string'},
            {name: 'age',    type: 'int'},
            {name: 'phone', type: 'string'},
            {name: 'email', type: 'string'},
            {name: 'alive', type: 'boolean', defaultValue: true}
      ]
  });
  var store = new Ext.data.Store({
      model: 'User',
      autoLoad: true,
      proxy: {
        type: 'ajax',
        url: 'users.json',
        reader: {
            type: 'json',
            root: 'users'
        }
      }
  });

    var form;

    var formBase = {
        scroll: 'vertical',
        items: [{
                    xtype: 'selectfield',
                    name : 'user',
                    label: 'User',
                    store: store,
                    valueField: 'name',
                    displayField: 'name'
                }]
    };

    if (Ext.is.Phone) {
```

```
            formBase.fullscreen = true;
        } else {
            Ext.apply(formBase, {
                autoRender: true,
                floating: true,
                modal: true,
                centered: true,
                hideOnMaskTap: false,
                height: 385,
                width: 480
            });
        }

        form = new Ext.form.FormPanel(formBase);
        form.show();
        }
    });
```

2. Update the `index.html` file.

3. Deploy and access it from the browser. You may also run it using the emulator.

How it works...

```
var store = new Ext.data.Store({
    model: 'User',
    autoLoad: true,
    proxy: {
      type: 'ajax',
      url: 'users.json',
      reader: {
            type: 'json',
            root: 'users'
      }
    }
});
```

Setting `type` to `ajax` sets up `AjaxProxy` on the store. Ajax proxy works only if the specified URL is in the domain in which the application is running. `users.json` contains the JSON formatted data that we saw in the *Converting incoming JSON data into models using JsonReader* recipe. As `data` represents a JSON format of the data, we configured the `json` type `reader` and used `root` to point to the property in the data which contains the actual user information.

See also

▸ The recipe named *Setting up the browser-based development environment* in *Chapter 1*

▸ The recipe named *Getting your form ready with FormPanel* in *Chapter 2*

▸ The recipe named *Working with the select field* in *Chapter 2*

▸ The recipe named *Working with Store* in this chapter

▸ The recipe named *Converting incoming JSON data into models using JsonReader* in this chapter

Sorting of the data

The store supports filters, sorting, and grouping. These are very important functionalities which make the Sencha Touch data classes so useful. One can sort data in one or more fields, apply one or more filter, and group the data on certain fields. All this is available on the client side, as well as the server side. On the client side, the framework applies the sorting, filtering, and grouping on the models stored within it whereas on server side, the information is passed to the remote server, so that the server-side application/script can handle them and provide the desired sorted, filtered, and grouped data.

In this recipe, we will see how to sort the data, send the sorting information to the server, and customize the information sent to the server.

Getting ready

Make sure that you have set up your development environment by following the recipes outlined in *Chapter 1*.

How to do it...

```
var store = new Ext.data.Store({
    model: 'User',
    autoLoad: true,
    proxy: {
      type: 'ajax',
      url: 'users.json',
      reader: {
          type: 'json',
          root: 'users'
      }
    }
});
```

```
store.sort([
    {
        property : 'age',
        direction: 'DESC'
    },
    {
        property : 'name',
        direction: 'ASC'
    }
]);
```

How it works...

The code in this recipe is based on the previous recipe, *Loading data through AJAX using AjaxProxy*. In the preceding code, we are using `AjaxProxy` to load data from the `users.json` file and using the `sort` method, we are sorting the data in the store:

```
store.sort([
    {
        property : 'age',
        direction: 'DESC'
    },
    {
        property : 'name',
        direction: 'ASC'
    }
]);
```

The `sort` method accepts an object containing `property` and sort `direction`. `property` instructs the model field on which record the sorting should be done and `direction` instructs whether the record should be sorted in ascending or descending order. The direction name is case sensitive and we should always use the uppercase versions.

As we have added sorting on two fields: `age` and `name`, the order of sorting is the order in which the sorting information is added. Therefore, in our case, the records will be first sorted on `age` and then on `name`.

There's more...

Alternatively, the sorting can happen on the server side. Let's see how to enable the server-side sorting and send the sorting information to the server, so that the server-side code can return the sorted data using the specified information.

Sending the sorting information to the server

We send the sorting information to the server so that the server-side application can sort the data before returning it to the client-side application. To ask the framework to send the sorting information to the server, we will have to set `remoteSort` to `true` on the store as follows:

```
var store = new Ext.data.Store({
    model: 'User',
    autoLoad: true,
    proxy: {
      type: 'ajax',
      url: 'users.php',
      reader: {
          type: 'json',
          root: 'users'
      },
      remoteSort: true


    }
});
```

Once this is set, the sorting information will be passed as part of the query parameter as shown in the following screenshot:

Customizing the sort information being sent to the server

By default, the sort information is sent to the server using the parameter named `sort`. If we want to change this default, then we use the `sortParam` property on `proxy` to set it to the desired name, say, `searchCritera`.

If we don't want the sorting information to be sent to the server, we can achieve it by setting the `sortParam` property to `undefined`.

See also

▶ The recipe named *Setting up the browser-based development environment* in Chapter 1

▶ The recipe named *Working with Store* in this chapter

▶ The recipe named *Loading data through AJAX using AjaxProxy* in this chapter

Data grouping

In this recipe, we will see how to group the data and how to send the grouping information to the server application.

Getting ready

Make sure that you have set up your development environment by following the recipes outlined in *Chapter 1*.

How to do it...

```
var store = new Ext.data.Store({
    model: 'User',
    autoLoad: true,
    proxy: {
      type: 'ajax',
      url: 'users.json',
      reader: {
          type: 'json',
          root: 'users'
      },
      remoteSort: true,
    groupField: 'age',
    groupDir: 'ASC'
    }
});
```

How it works...

The preceding code shows how to specify the grouping information and send it to the server. The related properties are `groupField` and `groupDir`. The `groupField` property instructs the model field on which data needs to be grouped and the `groupDir` property instructs the direction—ascending or descending. Grouping information is treated in a similar way to the sort information. Grouping information is passed as the first `sort` information.

See also

▶ The recipe named *Setting up the browser-based development* environment in *Chapter 1*

▶ The recipe named *Working with Store* in this chapter

▶ The recipe named *Loading data through AJAX using AjaxProxy* in this chapter

Filtering data

Filtering is a great way to remove unwanted records based on certain criteria. A store allows us to specify the filters and additional properties to send the filter information to the server application. One or more filters can be applied. In this recipe, we will see how to do this.

Getting ready

Make sure that you have set up your development environment by following the recipes outlined in *Chapter 1*.

How to do it...

The following code highlights the property and method that needs to be used in order to apply the filtering:

```
var store = new Ext.data.Store({
    model: 'User',
    autoLoad: true,
    proxy: {
      type: 'ajax',
      url: 'users.json',
      reader: {
          type: 'json',
          root: 'users'
      },
      remoteFilter: true
    }
});
```

```
store.filter([
    {
        property: 'name',
        value    : /Aj/
    }
]);
```

How it works...

The code in this recipe is based on the previous recipe, *Loading data through AJAX using AjaxProxy*. In the preceding code, we use `AjaxProxy` to load data from the `users.json` file and by using the `filter` method, we are filtering the data in the store:

```
store.filter([
    {
        property: 'name',
        value    : /Aj/
    }
]);
```

The `filter` method accepts an object containing `property` and `value` to compare with. `property` instructs the model field on which the filtering should be done and `value` instructs the value/pattern which shall be used to filter the records.

See also

▶ The recipe named *Setting up the browser-based development environment* in *Chapter 1*

▶ The recipe named *Working with Store* in this chapter

▶ The recipe named *Loading data through AJAX using AjaxProxy* in this chapter

Using a cross-domain URL in your application

Besides `AjaxProxy`, `ScriptTagProxy` is the other server proxy which helps us to persist the model on a remote server and load it from the same. The only catch is that this proxy is used only when the domain where the server is running is different from the domain where the application is running, for example, loading the search detail from the Google Custom search API. This recipe outlines the usage of `ScriptTagProxy` to make cross-domain URL calls.

Getting ready

Make sure that you have set up your development environment by following the recipes outlined in *Chapter 1*.

How to do it...

Carry out the following steps:

1. Create and open a new file named `ch05_14.js` and paste the following code into it:

```
Ext.setup({
    onReady: function() {
    Ext.regModel('SearchResult', {
        fields: [
            {name: 'kind',   type: 'string'},
            {name: 'title',    type: 'string'},
            {name: 'htmlTitle', type: 'string'},
            {name: 'displayLink', type: 'string'},
            {name: 'snippet', type: 'boolean', defaultValue: true}
        ]
    });

    var store = new Ext.data.Store({
      model: 'SearchResult',
      autoLoad: true,
      proxy: {
       type: 'scripttag',
       url: 'https://www.googleapis.com/customsearch/v1?key=' +
        'XXXXXXXX' + '&cx=013036536707430787589:_pqjad5hr1a&q=rose',
       reader: {
         type: 'json',
         root: 'items'
       }
      }
    });

    var form;

    var formBase = {
        scroll: 'vertical',
        items: [{
                xtype: 'selectfield',
                name : 'user',
                label: 'User',
                store: store,
                valueField: 'title',
                displayField: 'title'
```

```
                    }]
        };

        if (Ext.is.Phone) {
            formBase.fullscreen = true;
        } else {
            Ext.apply(formBase, {
                autoRender: true,
                floating: true,
                modal: true,
                centered: true,
                hideOnMaskTap: false,
                height: 385,
                width: 480
            });
        }

        form = new Ext.form.FormPanel(formBase);
        form.show();
        }
});
```

2. Update the `index.html` file.

3. Deploy and access it from the browser. You may also run it using the emulator. You will see a screen similar to the one shown in the following screenshot:

How it works...

In the preceding code, we have used the `scripttag` proxy to read search data from Google's search API.

```
var store = new Ext.data.Store({
    model: 'SearchResult',
    autoLoad: true,
    proxy: {
        type: 'scripttag',
        url: 'https://www.googleapis.com/customsearch/v1?key=' +
         'AIzaSyD8nxb7bFwURb6gXqHWz9dFMQw8-bZCvPw' +
         '&cx=013036536707430787589:_pqjad5hr1a&q=rose',
        reader: {
            type: 'json',
            root: 'items'
        }
    }
});
```

The Google API returns data in the form of JSON. The following screenshot shows the response received from the Google API call:

`items` contains the actual response data that we are interested in. Hence, `reader` is configured with `json type` and the `items` as the `root`.

See also

- ▸ The recipe named *Setting up the browser-based development environment* in *Chapter 1*
- ▸ The recipe named *Getting your form ready with FormPanel* in *Chapter 2*
- ▸ The recipe named *Working with the select field* in *Chapter 2*
- ▸ The recipe named *Working with Store* in this chapter

6
Adding the Components

In this chapter, we will cover:

- ► Working with Button
- ► Creating a sheet of buttons with ActionSheet
- ► Carousel
- ► Managing a list of data using List
- ► Grouping items in a List
- ► Navigating through a list of data using indexBar
- ► Working with a list of nested data using NestedList
- ► Picking your choice using Picker
- ► Switching between multiple views using SegmentedButton
- ► Working with Tab panels
- ► Quicker access to application features using Toolbar
- ► Creating a new component
- ► Extending an existing component capability
- ► Overriding a component behavior
- ► Adding behavior to an existing component using plugins

Introduction

So far, we have seen the usage of various components such as `FormPanel`, `DataView`, `Panel`, and so on. There were some components that we had used in previous recipes, such as toolbar, but not discussed in detail. Besides, there are some more components which are worth a discussion to understand the purpose of their existence and use them accordingly. In addition, this chapter goes beyond the existing components by covering how to create a new component, extending an existing component, and building plugins and using them in enhancing the capabilities of a component.

Working with Button

This recipe introduces the button component where it shows how to make use of the button in our application, how to have a different look-n-feel for it, and handle the user action.

Getting ready

Make sure that you have set up your development environment by following the recipes outlined in Chapter 1.

Create a new folder named `ch06` in the same folder where we had created `ch01` and `ch02` folders. We will be using this new folder to keep the code.

How to do it...

Carry out the following steps:

1. Create and open a new file named `ch06_01.js` and paste the following code in it:

```
Ext.setup({
  onReady: function() {

    var buttons = [
      {
        text: 'Normal',
        handler: function() {
          Ext.Msg.alert('Info', 'You have clicked: ' + this.text);
        }
      },
      {
        ui  : 'round',
        text: 'Round'
      },
```

```
      {
        ui   : 'small',
        text: 'Small'
      }
    ];

    var panel = new Ext.Panel({
      fullscreen: true,
        layout: {
            type : 'hbox',
            pack : 'center'
        },
        defaults: {
          xtype: 'button'
        },
        items: [buttons]
    });
    }
  });
```

2. Update `index.html` file.

3. Deploy and access it from the browser. You may also run it using the emulator.

How it works...

The preceding code creates a panel with three buttons laid out using the `hbox` layout. The following code defines `xtype` for all the items of the panel to `button`:

```
defaults: {
  xtype: 'button'
}
```

This short cut allows us to set `xtype` for all the children in one go.

The `ui` property defines the look-n-feel of the button. This acts as a short cut to a group of CSS styles.

The `handler` function is called when the button is clicked or tapped. It is equivalent to the handling of the tap event on the button.

There's more...

Additionally, the button component provides the mechanism to specify the badge and also uses the icons along with the text. The following section describes how to make use of these functionalities.

Using badge

Badge is a text which appears on top of the button. This may be useful to highlight a button with a badge, say, New, indicating to the user that this button is newly added. This helps us grab the user attention. The following code snippet shows how to show a badge with the New text on the button:

```
{
        ui   : 'round',
        text: 'Round',
        badgeText: 'New'

}
```

When we run the code, we will see the **Round** button with a badge with a **New** text, as shown in the following screenshot:

The framework uses the pre-defined CSS to show the badge. If you want to define and use a different style, you can do so by setting the badgeCls property on the button.

Using icon

It is generally considered good practice to use an icon along with the text while creating a button as it gives both textual, as well as visual meaning to it. People who have difficulty in reading and understanding the text may find it easier to remember the icon and understand it easily. For this, the button component supports multiple properties: icon, iconCls, and iconAlign. If you want to use the image directly as an icon, you can do it by setting the icon property. However, it is better that we define a CSS class and use it. For this, we shall use iconCls. The following code snippet shows the usage of these properties:

```
{
        ui   : 'small',
        text: 'Small',
        //icon: 'ch06/cancel.png',
        iconCls: 'cancel-icon',
        iconAlign: 'right'
}
```

iconAlign allows us to align the icon with respect to the text. The valid values are top, bottom, right, and left, where left is the default alignment. The following screenshot shows how the icon would appear on the button:

See also

The recipe named *Setting up the browser-based development environment* in *Chapter 1*

Creating a sheet of buttons with ActionSheet

In an application, say, on an entity, multiple actions can be performed. For example, on an inbox item, a user can reply back to the sender, reply to all, delete the mail, and view the complete mail. Moreover, these actions may vary based on the entity in the context. To handle such scenarios, the Sencha Touch framework provides an ActionSheet component, which allows us to show a sheet of buttons which can help the user trigger different actions. This recipe shows us how to create ActionSheet and use it in an application.

Getting ready

Make sure that you have set up your development environment by following the recipes outlined in *Chapter 1*.

How to do it...

Carry out the following steps:

1. Create and open a new file named ch06_02.js and copy the ch04/ch04_07.js content inside it.

2. Add the following code at the beginning of the onReady function:

```
var actionSheet = new Ext.ActionSheet({
  items: [
    {
      text: 'Cancel',
      ui  : 'decline',
      handler: function() {
        actionSheet.hide();
      }
```

```
      },
      {
        text: 'Detail',
        handler: function() {
          var recs = Ext.getCmp('images-data-view').
            getSelectedRecords();
          Ext.getCmp('detail-panel').update('<img src="' +
            recs[0].data.url + '" title="' +
            recs[0].data.title + '">');
          Ext.getCmp('images-view').
            getLayout().setActiveItem(1);
          Ext.getCmp('back-button').show();
          Ext.getCmp('rose-button').hide();
          Ext.getCmp('daffodil-button').hide();
          Ext.getCmp('hibiscus-button').hide();
          actionSheet.hide();
        }
      },
      {
        text: 'Delete',
        ui  : 'confirm',
        handler: function(){
          Ext.Msg.confirm("Confirmation", "Are you sure you want
                         to delete the picture?", function(btn){
            if (btn == "yes") {
              var dview = Ext.getCmp('images-data-view');
              var recs = dview.getSelectedRecords();
              dview.getStore().remove(recs);
            }
            actionSheet.hide();
          });
        }
      }
    ]
  });
```

3. Change the `selectionchange` handler as per the following code:

```
selectionchange: function(model, recs) {
  if (recs.length > 0) {
    actionSheet.show();
  }
},
```

4. Include the `ch04/ch04.css` file into `index.html`.

5. Update the `index.html` file.

6. Deploy and access it from the browser. You may also run it using the emulator. You shall see the flowers on the screen and when you click/tap on a particular flower, you will see the buttons docking in from left, as shown in the following screenshot:

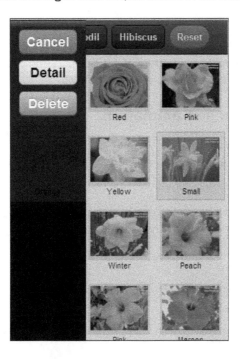

How it works...

The preceding code creates a sheet of three buttons: **Cancel**, **Detail**, and **Delete**. The `DataView` shows the photos and when a user selects a photo, the `selectionchange` event is fired and its handler shows the button sheet to the user by calling the `show` method on the `ActionSheet` instance.

On clicking the Cancel button, we are hiding the button sheet by calling the `hide` method. When the user clicks on the **Delete** button, the following handler code seeks the user confirmation and upon confirmation, removes the selected photo from the view's `store`.

```
Ext.Msg.confirm("Confirmation", "Are you sure you
    want to delete the picture?", function(btn){
    if (btn == "yes") {
      var dview = Ext.getCmp('images-data-view');
      var recs = dview.getSelectedRecords();
      dview.getStore().remove(recs);
```

```
        }
        actionSheet.hide();   //hide the sheet
    });
```

When the user clicks on the **Detail** button, the handler shows the bigger image of the selected photo, updates the toolbar to show the appropriate buttons, and hides the sheet.

There's more...

By default, the sheet appears at the bottom of the viewport and slides in and out when it is shown or hidden. Let us see how to change these defaults.

Change the position and animation

ActionSheet provides different properties to control these defaults:

- ▶ enter: It is the viewport side from which to anchor the sheet
- ▶ enterAnimation: The animation to be used

The following code snippet shows the usage of these fields to make sure that the sheet appears on the left-hand side and the animation it uses is fade:

```
var actionSheet = new Ext.ActionSheet({
    enter: 'left',
    enterAnimation: 'fade',
    items: [
        {
        ...
        ...
    }]
});
```

See also

- ▶ The recipe named *Setting up the browser-based development environment* in *Chapter 1*
- ▶ The recipe named *Building Custom Views* in *Chapter 4*

Carousel

Carousel is an extension of `Ext.Panel` and provides the ability to slide back and forth between different child items. Carousel, internally, uses the card layout to render items and allows the user to slide back and forth by setting the active item appropriately.

Getting ready

Make sure that you have set up your development environment by following the recipes outlined in *Chapter 1*.

How to do it...

Carry out the following steps:

1. Create and open a new file named ch06_03.js and paste the following code in it:

```
Ext.setup({
    onReady: function() {

        var actionSheet = new Ext.ActionSheet({
..........   //code is same as the one in previous recipe
..........   //code is same as the one in previous recipe
        });

        var data = [{
          album:'rose',
          url:'http://www.pictures.vg/vgflowers/400x300/
            flowers_pics_4870.jpg',
          title:'Rose 1',
          about:'Peach'},
.........   //code is same as the one in previous recipe
.........   //code is same as the one in previous recipe
    {

          album:'hibiscus',
          url:'http://www.pictures.vg/vgflowers/400x300/
            cflowers3224.jpg',
          title:'Hibiscus 1',
          about:'Bright Red'}];

        var store = new Ext.data.JsonStore({
          data: data,
          mode: 'local',
        fields: [
```

```
                'url', 'title','about'
            ]
        });

        var tpl = new Ext.XTemplate(
            '<tpl for=".">',
                '<div class="thumb-wrap" id="{title}">',
                '<div class="thumb"><img src="{url}" title="{title}">
                </div>',
                '<span>{about}</span></div>',
            '</tpl>',
            '<div class="x-clear"></div>'
        );



        var filter = function(criteria) {
          return store.filterBy(function(record, id){
            if (record.get('album') === criteria ||
                Ext.isEmpty(criteria))
              return true;
            else
              return false;
          });
        }

        var carousel = new Ext.Carousel({
            items: [
                {
                    id: 'detail-panel',
                    width: 400,
                    height: 300,
                    styleHtmlContent: true,
                    scroll: 'vertical'
                },
                {
                  html: '<h1 style="font-size:16px;"><b>About Roses
                        </b></h1><p>The leaves are borne alternately
                        on the stem. In most species they are 5 to 15
                        centimetres (2.0 to 5.9 in) long, pinnate,
                        with (3-) 5-9 (-13) leaflets and basal
                        stipules; the leaflets usually have a
                        serrated margin, and often a few small
                        prickles on the underside of the stem. Most
                        roses are deciduous but a few (particularly
                        from South east Asia) are evergreen or
                        nearly so.</p>'
```

```
                },
                {
                    html: '<h1 style="font-size:16px;"><b>Uses</b>
                            </h1><p>Roses are best known as ornamental
                            plants grown for their flowers in the garden
                            and sometimes indoors. They have been also
                            used for commercial perfumery and commercial
                            cut flower crops. Some are used as landscape
                            plants, for hedging and for other utilitarian
                            purposes such as game cover and slope
                            stabilization. They also have minor medicinal
                            uses.</p>'
                }
            ]
    });

    var pnl = new Ext.Panel({
        id:'images-view',
        ........   //code is same as the one in previous recipe
        ........   //code is same as the one in previous recipe
        items: [new Ext.DataView({
            id: 'images-data-view',
        ........   //code is same as the one in previous recipe
        ........   //code is same as the one in previous recipe
          }), carousel],
        dockedItems: [
                {
                    xtype: 'toolbar',
        ..........   //code is same as the one in previous recipe
        ..........   //code is same as the one in previous recipe
                }
            ]
    });

    }
  });
  });
```

2. Update the index.html file.

3. Deploy and access it from the browser. You may also run it using the emulator. You will see a screen similar to the one shown in the following screenshot:

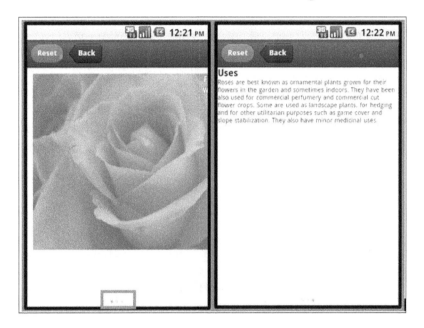

How it works...

The preceding code modifies the code in the previous recipe such that the panel to show the large photo is moved from the main panel to the Carousel. The Carousel has two more panels: **About** and **Uses** which contain more information about, say, roses.

The Ext.Carousel class implements the complete Carousel functionality. Internally, it uses the card layout to render its children.

There's more...

Orientation is one thing in Carousel, which different applications may have different needs. Some may like it to be horizontal whereas some may like it to be vertical. In the next section, we will see how to achieve it.

Changing the direction

By default, the Carousel direction is horizontal. Alternatively, if required, we can set it to vertical, as well. This behavior is provided by the `direction` property of the `Carousel` class. The following code snippet shows how to set this property on Carousel:

```
var carousel = new Ext.Carousel({
    direction: 'vertical',
      items: [
```

See also

▸ The recipe named *Setting up the browser-based development environment* in *Chapter 1*

▸ The recipe named *Building Custom Views* in *Chapter 4*

Managing a list of data using List

Say, in your application, there is a data set that needs to be presented to users in the form of a list, where users can scroll through the list and make their selection, for example, a list of contacts, list of places, list of matching words, and so on. Sencha Touch provides a `List` component to handle any list-related needs. This recipe shows how to use it to present the contact list to the user.

Getting ready

Make sure that you have set up your development environment by following the recipes outlined in *Chapter 1*.

How to do it...

Carry out the following steps:

1. Create and open a new file named `ch06_04.js` and paste the following code in it:

```
Ext.setup({
    onReady: function() {
Ext.regModel('Contact', {
    fields: ['firstName', 'lastName']
});

var store = new Ext.data.JsonStore({
    model   : 'Contact',
```

```
        data: [
            {firstName: 'Ajit',    lastName: 'Kumar'},
            {firstName: 'Alok',    lastName: 'Ranjan'},
            {firstName: 'Pradeep',lastName: 'Lavania'},
            {firstName: 'Sunil',   lastName: 'Kumar'},
            {firstName: 'Sujit',   lastName: 'Kumar'},
            {firstName: 'Pratyush',lastName: 'Kumar'},
            {firstName: 'Piyush', lastName: 'Kumar'},
            {firstName: 'Priti', lastName: ''},
            {firstName: 'Seema',   lastName: 'Singh'},
            {firstName: 'Ayush',   lastName: 'Kumar'},
            {firstName: 'Ayush',   lastName: 'Ranjan'},
            {firstName: 'Alisha', lastName: 'Lavania'},
            {firstName: 'Deepak',   lastName: 'Sinha'},
            {firstName: 'Sheela',   lastName: 'Kejawani'},
            {firstName: 'Srikanth',    lastName: 'Reddy'},
            {firstName: 'Suman', lastName: 'Ravuri'},
            {firstName: 'Ranjit', lastName: ''},
            {firstName: 'Jay',    lastName: 'Sharma'}
        ]
    });

    var list = new Ext.List({
        itemTpl: '<tpl for="."><div class="contact">{firstName}
                <strong>{lastName}</strong></div></tpl>',

        store: store,

        floating     : true,
        width        : 350,
        height       : 370,
        centered     : true,
        modal        : true,
        hideOnMaskTap: false
    });
    list.show();
        }
    });
```

2. Update the `index.html` file.

3. Deploy and access it from the browser. You may also run it using the emulator. You will see the following screen:

How it works...

The preceding code creates a list of contact names and allows the user to select an entry.

```
Ext.regModel('Contact', {
    fields: ['firstName', 'lastName']
});
```

This code registers a `Contact` model with the model manager. The model is used on the store in conjunction with the `data` array to convert the `data` array into the model and populate the store.

`List` extends `DataView`. Thus, it inherits the capabilities and behaviors of `DataView`. The view is refreshed as soon as the models are loaded into the store, which is associated with the list. Each record in the list is rendered using the template defined in `itemTpl`.

There's more...

Sorting is one need that arises naturally when we are dealing with the list information. Let us see how we can have a sorted data inside a list.

Sorting entries

In order to sort entries in the list, the list does not provide any method. Rather, we shall set up `sorters` on the associated `store`, as shown in the following code snippet:

```
var store = new Ext.data.JsonStore({
    model  : 'Contact',
    sorters: 'firstName',
```

`sorters: 'firstName'` will sort the records by their first name and in the ascending order. If we want to sort the data on multiple fields and specify the specific way (ascending/descending) the data needs to be sorted, then we will expand the `sorters` property value to:

```
sorters: [{property: 'firstName', direction: 'ASC'},
          {property: 'lastName', direction: 'DESC'}],
```

See also

- ▶ The recipe named *Setting up browser-based development environment* in *Chapter 1*
- ▶ The recipe named *Working with Store* in *Chapter 5*

Grouping items in a List

In a list, you may want to see items grouped on certain criteria, for example, in our contact list, we may want to see our names grouped alphabetically. For this, the list allows us to group the data using the criteria and this recipe will show exactly how this can be achieved.

Getting ready

Make sure that you have setup your development environment by following the recipes outlined in *Chapter 1*.

How to do it...

Carry out the following steps:

1. Create and open a new file named `ch06_05.js` and paste the following code in it:

```
var list = new Ext.List({
    itemTpl: '<tpl for="."><div class="contact">{firstName}
            <strong>{lastName}</strong></div></tpl>',
    grouped    : true,
    store: store,

    floating   : true,
    width      : 350,
    height     : 370,
    centered   : true,
    modal      : true,
    hideOnMaskTap: false
});

var store = new Ext.data.JsonStore({
    model   : 'Contact',

    getGroupString : function(record) {
        return record.get('firstName')[0];
    },
....    //code from ch06_04.js
```

2. Update the `index.html` file.

3. Deploy and access it from the browser. You may also run it using the emulator. You will see the following screen:

How it works...

The preceding code builds on top of the code mentioned in the previous recipe. It adds the grouping capability to the list by setting the `grouped` property on the list to `true` and implementing a method `getGroupString` on the store, which is called by the framework to group the information as per the specified field, in this case, `firstName`. In the code, we are returning the first character of the first name from `getGroupString` and hence the data will be grouped on the returned character. However, we can group the data using the entire first name by returning the value of the `firstName` field by changing the function body to `return record.get('firstName')`

See also

- ▶ The recipe named *Setting up the browser-based development environment* in *Chapter 1*
- ▶ The recipe named *Working with Store* in *Chapter 5*
- ▶ The recipe named *Data grouping* in *Chapter 5*
- ▶ The recipe named *Managing a list of data using List* in this chapter

Navigating through a list of data using indexBar

Imagine there is big book that we are reading and we want to quickly locate the topic of our interest. The very first thing that we look forward to is the Index page which can tell us the topics and their page numbers. Similarly, in a list, if items are huge, we can use the index bar functionality to quickly go to the item of our choice, and this recipe will walk us through the step.

Getting ready

Make sure that you have set up your development environment by following the recipes outlined in *Chapter 1*.

How to do it...

Carry out the following steps:

1. Create and open a new file named ch06_06.js and paste the following code in it:

```
var list = new Ext.List({
    itemTpl: '<tpl for="."><div class="contact">{firstName}
            <strong>{lastName}</strong></div></tpl>',
    grouped     : true,
    indexBar    : true,   //use IndexBar
    store     : store,
    floating    : true,
    width       : 350,
    height      : 370,
    centered    : true,
    modal       : true,
    hideOnMaskTap: false
});
..... //code from ch06_04.js
```

2. Update the `index.html` file.

3. Deploy and access it from the browser. You may also run it using the emulator. You will see the following screen:

How it works...

In the preceding code, the index bar is enabled by setting the property `indexBar` to `true` on `List`. This property instructs the framework to generate an index bar (similar to the index at the end of the book) with A-Z alphabets and allows the user to jump to the matching entries when he/she clicks on a particular index.

See also

▶ The recipe named *Setting up the browser-based development environment* in *Chapter 1*

▶ The recipe named *Working with Store* in *Chapter 5*

▶ The recipe named *Managing a list of data using List* in this chapter

Working with a list of nested data using NestedList

Imagine you have a nested data structure which you would like to present to the user in the form of a list and allow him/her to drill down the nested data structure. In this recipe, we will understand how to achieve this using the `NestedList` component.

Getting ready

Make sure that you have set up your development environment by following the recipes outlined in *Chapter 1*.

How to do it...

Carry out the following steps:

1. Create and open a new file named `ch06_07.js` and paste the following code in it:

```
Ext.setup({
    onReady: function() {
    var data = {
        items: [{
            text: 'Flowers',
            items: [{
                text: 'Roses',
                items: [{
                    text: 'Red',
                    leaf: true
                },{
                    text: 'Peach',
                    leaf: true
                },{
                    text: 'Yellow',
                    leaf: true
                }]
            },{
                text: 'Daffodils',
                leaf: true
            },{
                text: 'Hibiscus',
                leaf: true
            }]
        },{
```

```
                        text: 'Animals',
                        items: [{
                            text: 'Lion',
                            leaf: true
                        },{
                            text: 'Elephant',
                            leaf: true
                        }]
                    },{
                        text: 'Birds',
                        items: [{
                            text: 'Eagle',
                            leaf: true
                        },{
                            text: 'Hamsa',
                            leaf: true
                        },{
                            text: 'Pegion',
                            leaf: true
                        }]
                    }]
                };
                Ext.regModel('ListItem', {
                    fields: [{name: 'text', type: 'string'}]
                });
                var store = new Ext.data.TreeStore({
                    model: 'ListItem',
                    root: data,
                    proxy: {
                        type: 'ajax',
                        reader: {
                            type: 'tree',
                            root: 'items'
                        }
                    }
                });
                var nestedList = new Ext.NestedList({
                    fullscreen: true,
                    title: 'Fauna & Flora',
                    store: store
                });
                }
            });
```

2. Update the `index.html` file.

3. Deploy and access it from the browser. You may also run it using the emulator. You will see the following screen:

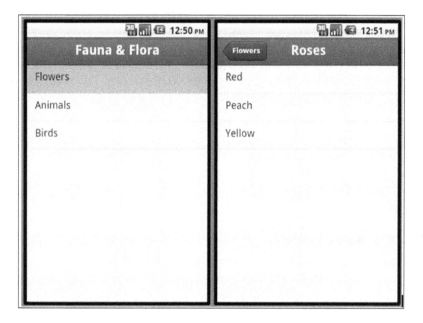

How it works...

The preceding code creates a `NestedList` component using the `data` array. The `NestedList` uses a `TreeStore`, which expects the data to follow a particular tree structure. The data structure shows that at the top level, `data` has three nodes: **Flowers**, **Animals**, and **Birds**. Each one of them has child items, for example, **Flowers** has immediate children **Roses**, **Daffodils**, and **Hibiscus**. For **Daffodils** and **Hibiscus**, the `leaf` property is set to `true`, indicating that they are the leaf nodes of the tree and will not have any child items. The nesting can go up to any level. Each node has a property `text`, which the `TreeStore` uses to show them on the screen.

`NestedList` extends the `Panel` component, and based on the nesting of the data and at what level the user is, it creates a docked toolbar at the top and displays buttons on the toolbar to allow the user to navigate through the hierarchy. The button labels are generated using the `text` property of the nodes.

There's more...

There are additional features available with a tab panel and the subsequent sections cover them.

Using a property other than text

By default, the `NestedList` uses the `text` property of the node to display it on the screen and generate the button labels. If our data has a different property, say, `label`, then we shall use the `displayField` property on `NestedList` and set it to `'label'`, as follows:

```
var nestedList = new Ext.NestedList({
        fullscreen: true,
        title: 'Fauna & Flora',
        displayField: 'label',
        store: store
});
```

Showing the Back button

Say, in our application, we want to have a label **Back** for the button rather than the text of the parent node of the current level. This can be achieved by setting the `useTitleAsBackText` to `false`.

No toolbar, please!

By default, `NestedList` generates a toolbar at the top, adds a **Back** button to it, and handles the click event on it. If we do not want to see this toolbar, we shall set the `useToolbar` property on `NestedList` to `false`.

See also

The recipe named *Setting up the browser-based development environment* in *Chapter 1*

Picking your choice using Picker

In *Chapter 2*, we had talked about `DatePicker`, which shows the dates in the form of slots and allows us to pick a date. `DatePicker` is a specialised version of the `Picker` class. In this recipe, we will see how to make use of this class.

Getting ready

Make sure that you have set up your development environment by following the recipes outlined in *Chapter 1*.

How to do it...

Carry out the following steps:

1. Create and open a new file named `ch06_08.js` and paste the following code in it:

```
Ext.setup({
    onReady: function() {
var picker = new Ext.Picker({
    slots: [
        {
            name : 'color',
            data : [
              {text: 'Red', value: 'red'},
              {text: 'Peach', value: 'peach'},
              {text: 'Yellow', value: 'yellow'},
              {text: 'White', value: 'white'}
            ]
        }
    ],
    listeners: {
      pick: function(picker, pickedObj, slot) {
        Ext.Msg.alert('Info', 'Value picked is: ' +
                    pickedObj.color);
      }
    }
});

picker.show();
    }
});
```

2. Update the `index.html` file.

3. Deploy and access it from the browser. You may also run it using the emulator. You will see the following screen:

How it works...

The preceding code creates a picker to allow the user to choose a color of their choice. Each color detail is added as a slot to the picker. Every slot contains two properties; `text` and `value`. The `text` property is used to display the name in the slot and `value` is given back to the program when the user picks up a slot.

We then register a handler for the `pick` event on the picker. The handler is fired when the user selects a slot. The parameter `pickerObj` contains the information about the slot that is selected. This object contains the `name` of the slots as its property and the value of the selected slot is set as its value. In our case, the `pickerObj` will look like this when the user selects the **Peach** slot:

```
{
    color: "peach"
}
```

There's more...

Like any other component, there are certain defaults defined by `Picker` and for all practical purposes. We may have to deviate from them, for example, the position, animation, and alignment. The following section shows how to do this.

Changing the position and animation

The `Picker` class extends `Sheet` and inherits the positioning and animation properties from it. We can use the four properties: `enter`, `exit`, `enterAnimation`, and `exitAnimation` to indicate the position of the picker with respect to the viewport when it is shown or hidden and the kind of animation that shall be used. The following code snippet shows the usage of these properties to show the picker on the top of the screen and uses the `fade` animation when it is being shown and `flip` when it is hidden:

```
var picker = new Ext.Picker({
  enter: 'top',
  enterAnimation: 'fade',
  exit: 'top',
  exitAnimation: 'flip',
```

By default, the picker uses the `bottom` position and `slid` animation.

Aligning the slot text

By default, the slot shows the text in the center. However, by using the `align` property on slots, we can left/right align the texts as follows:

```
    slots: [
        {
            name : 'color',
            align: 'left',
```

See also

The recipe named *Setting up the browser-based development environment* in *Chapter 1*

Switching between multiple views using SegmentedButton

This recipe describes the usage of the `SegmentedButton` component, which is generally a part of the toolbar and is useful in switching between different views.

Make sure that you have set up your development environment by following the recipes outlined in *Chapter 1*.

How to do it...

1. Create and open a new file named `ch06_09.js` and paste the following code in it:

```
Ext.setup({
    onReady: function() {
    var segmentedButton = new Ext.SegmentedButton({
        renderTo: Ext.getBody(),
        items: [
          {
            text: 'Album'
          },
          {
            text    : 'About',
            pressed: true
          },
          {
            text: 'Help'
          }
        ],
        listeners: {
          toggle: function(container, button, pressed){
            console.log("User toggled the '" + button.text + "'
                        button: " + (pressed ? 'on' : 'off'));
          }
        }
    });
    }
});
```

2. Update the `index.html` file.

3. Deploy and access it from the browser. You may also run it using the emulator. You will see the following screen:

Album	About	Help

How it works...

The preceding code creates a `SegmentedButton` with three buttons: **Album**, **About**, and **Help** and allows the user to select one of them. Setting `pressed: true` on the **About** button ensures that it will be selected, by default. A selected button is de-selected only if the user selects another button.

The `SegmentedButton` component fires the `toggle` event every time a button is selected and de-selected. Our handler for the toggle event shows a message informing us which button is selected/de-selected. For example, when the **Album** button is pressed, we see two messages appearing in the console: one, saying **About button: off** and other one, saying **Album button: on**

`renderTo` is the property where we specify the element whose child the item would become. In this example, we have specified the document body, which is returned by the `Ext.getBody()` method to instruct the Touch framework that the segmented button shall be rendered to the document body.

There's more...

Segmented button also allows us to press multiple buttons. Let's see how to do it.

Multiple pressed buttons

If we need the capability to keep multiple buttons pressed, we can achieve it by setting the `allowMultiple` property to `true`. Setting this property allows us to de-select an already selected button.

See also

The recipe named *Setting up the browser-based development environment* in *Chapter 1*

Working with Tab panels

The Tab panel is a popular UI component which can hold other components and that can be accessed in a tabbed fashion using a tab bar. In this recipe, we will learn about the tab panel and the different options that we may use to build our application.

Getting ready

Make sure that you have set up your development environment by following the recipes outlined in *Chapter 1*.

How to do it...

1. Create and open a new file named `ch06_10.js` and paste the following code in it:

```
Ext.setup({
    onReady: function() {

  new Ext.TabPanel({
    fullscreen: true,
    ui        : 'light',
    sortable  : true,
    items: [
      {
        title: 'Album',
        html: 'Contains the photos!',
        cls: 'tab1'
      },
      {
        title: 'Help',
        html: '<h1 style="font-size:16px;"><b>Help</b></h1><p>This
               application shows the album of flower pictures.
               You can filter the flowers based on their
               category, e.g. Rose, and view the additional
               detail about them.</p>',
        cls  : 'tab2'
      },
      {
        title: 'About',
        html : '<h1 style="font-size:16px;"><b>About this
                app!</b></h1><p>Version 0.1</p>',
        cls  : 'tab3'
      }
    ]
  });
    }
});
```

2. Update the `index.html` file.

3. Deploy and access it from the browser. You may also run it using the emulator. You shall see the following screen:

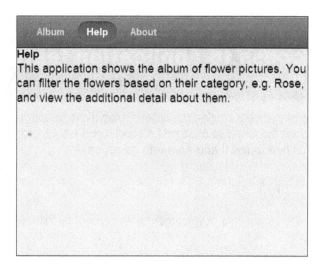

How it works...

The preceding code creates a tab panel with three panels. Internally, the tab panel generates a tab bar using the title of each panel item and with that, it allows the user to switch between different tabs.

There's more...

There are other interesting options available with the tab panel and the following section describes them.

Positioning the tab bar at the bottom

By default, the tab bar is positioned on the top. In order to show it at the bottom, we shall set the `tabBarDock` property to `bottom`.

Card switch animation

By default, the tab panel uses the `slide` animation. This can be changed by setting the `cardSwitchAnimation` to the animation of your choice, such as `flip`.

The recipe named *Setting up the browser-based development environment* in *Chapter 1*

Quicker access to application features using Toolbar

Toolbar is a great way of getting a single-click access to application features. It can have buttons, drop-downs, text field, and so on. Sencha Touch provides a toolbar component and this recipe will show us how to use it and work with its options.

Getting ready

Make sure that you have set up your development environment by following the recipes outlined in *Chapter 1*.

How to do it...

Carry out the following steps:

1. Create and open a new file named ch06_11.js and paste the following code in it:

```
Ext.setup({
    onReady: function() {
var myToolbar = new Ext.Toolbar({

        title: 'My Toolbar',
        items: [
          {
            text: 'Rose'
          },
          {
            text: 'Daffodil'
          },{
            text: 'Hibiscus'
          },{
            text: 'Reset',
            ui: 'decline-round'
          }, {
            text: 'Back',
            ui: 'back'
          }
        ]
```

```
    });

    var myPanel = new Ext.Panel({
        dockedItems: [myToolbar],
        fullscreen : true,
        html       : 'Test Panel'
    });


    }
});
```

2. Update the `index.html` file.
3. Deploy and access it from the browser. You may also run it using the emulator. You will see the following screen:

How it works...

The preceding code creates a toolbar with five buttons inside it and the toolbar is added to the panel. The **Reset** button is using `decline-round` as the `ui` and the **Back** button is using `back` as `ui` for a different look and feel.

There's more...

What if we want to have non-button components in our toolbar? Let us see.

Adding non-button components

The `defaultType` config property on the toolbar defines the `xtype` that shall be used for each item being added to it. Unless the `xtype` is specified on an item, `xtype` is defaulted to `button`, which is the default value for `defaultType`. This is the reason we did not have to specify the `xtype` for buttons, in the preceding code. In order to add a component of other `xtype`, we will have to set the `xtype` property on the particular item. For example, the following code shows adding a select field to the toolbar:

```
items: [{
  xtype: 'selectfield'
}, {
  text: 'Rose'
}]
```

The recipe named *Setting up the browser-based development environment* in *Chapter 1*

Creating a new component

So far, we have seen various components which the Sencha Touch framework offers and how to use them to model our application. However, for all practical reasons, there may be a need to create new components or extend the capability of an existing component. This recipe walks us through the steps to create a new component.

Getting ready

Make sure that you have set up your development environment by following the recipes outlined in *Chapter 1*.

How to do it...

Carry out the following steps:

1. Create and open a new file named `PhotoAlbum.js` and paste the following code in it:

```
Ext.ns('Touch.book.ux');

Touch.book.ux.PhotoAlbum = Ext.extend(Ext.DataView, {
  tpl : new Ext.XTemplate(
        '<tpl for=".">',
            '<div class="thumb-wrap" id="{title}">',
            '<div class="thumb"><img src="{url}"
                title="{title}"></div>',
            '<span>{about}</span></div>',
        '</tpl>',
        '<div class="x-clear"></div>'
    ),
    scroll: 'vertical',
    autoHeight:true,
    singleSelect: true,
    overItemCls:'x-view-over',
    itemSelector:'div.thumb-wrap',,
    emptyText: 'No images to display',
    monitorOrientation: true,
  initComponent: function() {
```

```
      this.addListener('selectionchange', function(model, recs) {
        if (recs.length > 0) {
          Ext.Msg.alert('Info', 'Selected: ' +
            recs[0].data.album + ' : ' + recs[0].data.about);
        }
                });

      this.addListener('orientationchange', function(model, recs) {
                pnl.refresh();
                });

      Touch.book.ux.PhotoAlbum.superclass.initComponent.apply(this);
    },

  onRender: function(container, position) {
    this.store.loadData(this.data);

    Touch.book.ux.PhotoAlbum.superclass.onRender.apply
      (this, arguments);
  }
});

    Ext.reg('photoalbum', Touch.book.ux.PhotoAlbum);
```

2. Create and open a new file named ch06_12.js and paste the following code in it:

```
Ext.setup({
    onReady: function() {

    var data = [{
        album:'rose',
        url:'http://www.pictures.vg/vgflowers/400x300/
          flowers_pics_4870.jpg',
        title:'Rose 1',
        about:'Peach'},
        .........
        .........
    {
        album:'hibiscus',
        url:'http://www.pictures.vg/vgflowers/400x300/
          cflowers3224.jpg',
        title:'Hibiscus 1',
        about:'Bright Red'}];

    var store = new Ext.data.JsonStore({
        mode: 'local',
```

```
        fields: [
            'url', 'title','about'
        ]
    });

    var photoPnl = new Touch.book.ux.PhotoAlbum({
        data: data,
        store: store
    });

    var pnl = new Ext.Panel({
      id:'images-view',
        fullscreen: true,
        scroll: false,
        monitorOrientation: true,
        defaults: {
            border: false
        },
        items: [photoPnl]
    });


    }
});
```

3. Update the index.html file.

4. Deploy and access it from the browser. You may also run it using the emulator.

How it works...

In the preceding code, we defined a new component PhotoAlbum in the Touch.book.ux namespace. PhotoAlbum extends the DataView component and defines its own template to render its items, and other common properties are defined inside it. The Ext.extend method provides us a way to define a new component by extending an existing one. You may also extend Object using this method. Additionally, two methods have been added to it: initComponent and onRender. These methods act as a hook into the overall component management lifecycle of Sencha Touch, which is out of this book's scope.

The initComponent method is called by the component manager to give a chance to the component to take care of its specific initialization. This is called during the initialization of a component. Our PhotoAlbum component registers the handlers for selectionchange and orientationchange events.

`onRender` is called during the rendering of the component and all our component is doing is loading `store` with the data as it is required to show the content.

The last statement, in both the methods, is calling the corresponding method of the super class, which is `DataView`. This is required, so that the parent class is initialized properly.

The `Ext.lib.Component` class contains the code related to the component lifecycle and understanding that may give you more insight into writing your own component.

The properties `tpl`, `scroll`, and so on which are being set inside the component, can be overridden by the value specified by the user at the time of constructing an instance of the `PhotoAlbum`. For example, if you want to have a different template for the `PhotoAlbum`, then you can pass the `tpl` property during the instantiation as follows:

```
New Touch.book.ux.PhotoAlbum({tpl: ….});
```

See also

▸ The recipe named *Setting up the browser-based development environment* in *Chapter 1*

▸ The recipe named *Working with Stores* in *Chapter 5*

Extending an existing component capability

In the previous recipe, we defined a new component and used it in our application. However, in some cases, the choice may not be to define a new component. Rather, we may have to see if we can add a capability to the existing component. For example, `String` is a standard object in JavaScript and we would like to add a new method—`formatWithWordBreak`—so that once it is added, it is available to the complete application code to make use of this new method without defining a `MyString` class and using it wherever we need `formatWithWordBreak`. This recipe will take us through the steps to achieve this requirement.

Getting ready

Make sure that you have set up your development environment by following the recipes outlined in *Chapter 1*.

How to do it...

Carry out the following steps:

1. Create and open a new file named `ch06_13.js` and paste the following code in it:

```
Touch.book.ux.PhotoAlbum.prototype.loadData = function(data) {
    this.store.loadData(data);
};


Ext.setup({
    onReady: function() {

    var data = [{
        album:'rose',
        url:'http://www.pictures.vg/vgflowers/400x300/
          flowers_pics_4870.jpg',
        title:'Rose 1',
        about:'Peach'},
        .........
        .........
{
        album:'hibiscus',
        url:'http://www.pictures.vg/vgflowers/400x300/
          cflowers3224.jpg',
        title:'Hibiscus 1',
        about:'Bright Red'}];
    var store = new Ext.data.JsonStore({
        mode: 'local',
        fields: [
            'url', 'title','about'
        ]
    });

    var photoPnl = new Touch.book.ux.PhotoAlbum({
        data: data,
        store: store
    });

    var pnl = new Ext.Panel({
      id:'images-view',
      fullscreen: true,
      scroll: false,
      monitorOrientation: true,
      defaults: {
```

```
        border: false
      },
      items: [photoPnl],
      dockedItems: [{
        xtype: 'toolbar',
        dock: 'top',
        items:[{
          text: 'Load New Data',
          handler: function() {
            photoPnl.loadData(newData);
          }
        }]
      }]
    });
    }
  });
```

2. Update the `index.html` file.

3. Deploy and access it from the browser. You may also run it using the emulator. You will see the following screen:

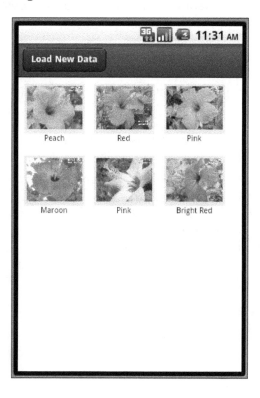

`prototype` is the standard JavaScript mechanism to extend an existing Java Script object, for example, adding the `printWithLineBreak` method to the exiting `String` class, so that the new method is accessible across the application code. The book *JavaScript: The Good Parts* by *Douglas Crockford* is an excellent resource on JavaScript. The preceding code uses the same mechanism to add a new method `loadData` to the existing `PhotoAlbum`, which loads data into the data view store. When the user clicks on the **Load New Data** button, `photoPnl` is loaded with the new data array by calling the newly added `loadData` method on the `PhotoAlbum` class.

See also

- ▶ The recipe named *Setting up browser-based development environment* in *Chapter 1*
- ▶ The recipe named *Creating a new component* in this chapter

Overriding a component behavior

This recipe will show us how to override an existing behavior of an existing component and use the modified behavior in the code.

Getting ready

Make sure that you have set up your development environment by following the recipes outlined in *Chapter 1*.

How to do it...

1. Create and open a new file named `PhotoAlbumOverride.js` and paste the following code in it:

```
Ext.override(Touch.book.ux.PhotoAlbum, {
  loadData : function(data) {
    if (this.store.getCount() > 0) {
      Ext.Msg.alert('Info', 'The view is already loaded with
                            data. No action will be performed.');
    } else {
      this.store.loadData(data);
    }
  }
});
```

2. Update the `index.html` file. We will use the existing `ch06_13.js` file.

3. Deploy and access it from the browser. You may also run it using the emulator. You will see the following screen:

How it works...

The `Ext.override` method allows us to override an existing behavior of a class. `Ext.override` allows us to override class properties and/or methods in a convenient way using the Touch API programming model. The good part is that you don't have to define a new class. Rather, you can override a property or a method of the class and still continue to use it with a different behavior. The method checks if there is already data loaded into the view and if so, it shows a message to the user and skips the loading of the new data. Otherwise, it loads the new data.

- The recipe named *Setting up the browser-based development environment* in *Chapter 1*
- The recipe named *Creating a new component* in this chapter
- The recipe named *Extending an existing component capability* in this chapter

Adding behavior to an existing component using plugins

Plugin is another mechanism by which we can enhance/customize the behavior of an existing component. The new behavior is effective only if the plugin is added to the component. Otherwise, the base behavior remains intact. In this recipe, we will understand how to create a new plugin and use that on an existing component.

Getting ready

Make sure that you have set up your development environment by following the recipes outlined in *Chapter 1*.

How to do it...

Carry out the following steps:

1. Create and open a new file `PhotoAlbumPlugIn.js` and paste the following code in it:

```
Touch.book.ux.PhotoAlbumPlugIn = Ext.extend(Ext.util.Observable, {

  init: function(viewCmp) {
    viewCmp.tpl = new Ext.XTemplate(
        '<tpl for=".">',
            '<div class="thumb-wrap" id="{title}">',
            '<div class="thumb"><img src="{url}"
                title="{title}"></div>',
            '<span>{title}</span></div>',
        '</tpl>',
        '<div class="x-clear"></div>'
    );
  }

});
```

2. Copy `ch06_13.js` as `ch06_15.js` and make the following changes to `photoPnl`:

```
var photoPnl = new Touch.book.ux.PhotoAlbum({
    data: data,
    store: store,
    plugins: [new Touch.book.ux.PhotoAlbumPlugIn()]
});
```

3. Update the `index.html` file.

4. Deploy and access it from the browser. You may also run it using the emulator. You will see the following screen:

How it works...

The Sencha Touch framework provides support for plugins and most of the components have a `plugins` property which can accept one or more plugins that need to be initialized for the component. Plugins is a great way to enhance the capabilities of a component without modifying its core behavior, for example, using a plugin to make the label editable for `DataView`. In the preceding code, we defined a plugin `PhotoAlbumPlugIn` within the `Touch.book.ux` namespace. The plugin extends the `Ext.util.Observable` class, so that if we have to deal with the events, our plugin would be capable of doing it. However, it is not mandatory to extend `Observable`. You may also extend `Object` to define a plugin. The important thing is that a plugin must have an `init` method defined which accepts the component reference to which the plugin was added to its `plugins` property. In our case, our plugin gets the reference to `PhotoAlbum` and sets `tpl` to a new template.

After the plugin is defined, `plugins: [new Touch.book.ux.PhotoAlbumPlugIn()]` associates the plugin with the `PhotoAlbum` and thus when the application is run, we see the template set by the plugin is used.

 A plugin is initialized after `initComponent` of the component is called. Therefore, you can be assured that when your plugin code is running, the complete component has been initialized.

See also

▶ The recipe named *Setting up the browser-based development environment* in *Chapter 1*

▶ The recipe named *Creating a new component* in this chapter

7
Adding Audio/Visual Appeal

In this chapter, we will cover:

- ► Animate me!
- ► Ding-dong! You have a message!
- ► Working with videos
- ► Adding charting support to your app
- ► Working with an area chart
- ► Generating a bar chart
- ► Creating a column chart
- ► Showing a group of bars and columns
- ► Switching between stacked and grouped orientation
- ► Highlighting and displaying an item detail
- ► Creating a gauge chart
- ► Creating a line chart
- ► Creating a pie chart
- ► Rotating the pies
- ► Grouping the pies
- ► Highlighting a pie
- ► Using a radar chart
- ► Using a scatter chart

Introduction

So far, we have worked with components which present the data either in the form of lists or form field or custom views. However, there is always a need in an application to present the information visually. In addition, notification is another key need in an application where you want to notify the user that a certain event has occurred in the system, for example, a new sales inquiry has arrived, an approval request has come for your approval, and so on. This chapter starts with introducing animation where we will see how to animate the elements in Sencha Touch and the different types of in-built animations supported by the framework. Next, we will see how to use the audio control in our application to have notifications, audio help, and so on. After audio, we will look into the video component and see how to use them in our application. In the subsequent recipes, we will learn how to set up the charts support in our application, what are the different types of charts available with the framework, how to use them, and also understand the ways to build interactive charts, which can respond to user actions.

Animate me!

A Sencha Touch application is built using the elements, represented by `Ext.Element`, and every element of it can be animated. In this recipe, we will see how to animate an element, what are the available types of animations, and how to change the animation properties.

Getting ready

Make sure that you have set up your development environment by following the recipes outlined in *Chapter 1*.

Create a new folder named `ch07` in the same folder where we had created `ch01` and `ch02` folders. We will be using this new folder to keep the code.

How to do it...

Carry out the following steps:

1. Create and open a new file named `ch07_01.js` and paste the following code into it:

```
Ext.setup({
    onReady: function() {
  var pnl = new Ext.Panel({
      renderTo: Ext.getBody(),
      style: 'background-color:gold;',
      height: 100,
      width: 100,
```

```
    });

    Ext.Anim.run(pnl.getEl(), 'cube', {

    });

        }
    });
```

2. Update the `index.html` file.

3. Deploy and access it from the browser or the device of your choice.

How it works...

In the preceding code, we created a panel instance, which was rendered to the document body. After its instantiation, we animated the panel by calling the `run` method of the `Ext.Anim` class. The first argument to the `run` method indicates which element needs to be animated, the second argument—`'cube'`—indicates the type of animation that needs to be applied to the element, and the third argument is used to pass the animation specific configuration object, which is, in this case, empty. This means that the default configuration will be applied.

The list of animations supported by Sencha Touch is defined in the `Ext.anims` class and the list is as follows:

- ► cube
- ► fade
- ► flip
- ► pop
- ► slide
- ► wipe

Internally, each animation type corresponds to some calculation and then uses the appropriate Webkit CSS properties to animate the element. A list of Webkit CSS properties can be found at `http://css-infos.net/properties/webkit.php`

There's more...

In the previous code, we saw that the third argument to the `run` method is the animation-specific configuration. There are various options that can be passed, which are outlined in the `Ext.Anim` class. Let us look at some of the important ones.

Working with different animation durations

By default, 250 millisecond is the animation duration. If this is not the desired one, then we can change it by passing the `duration` config option to the `run` method. `duration` accepts a value in milliseconds. The following code snippet shows how to pass the `duration`:

```
Ext.Anim.run(pnl.getEl(), 'cube', {
   duration : 2000  //20 seconds

});
```

Direction of animation

Most of the animations use a default direction for their animation. It is useful in deciding the side from which the element will enter into the scene; for example, the `cube` animation uses the `left` direction, by default. We can change this by passing the `direction` config to the `run` method. Possible values are:

- `left`
- `right`
- `up`
- `down`

Reversing the animation

If we want to reverse the direction of animation, it can be done by setting the `reverse` property to `true` and passing the same to the `run` method.

Postponing animation

If we don't want the animation to start immediately but want it to start after a certain amount of time, then we can achieve it by using the `delay` option. The `delay` option accepts a value in milliseconds.

See also

The recipe named *Setting up the browser-based development environment* in *Chapter 1*

Ding-dong! You have a message!

Say, we are building an application for the sales force which allows them to look at the orders placed in the ERP system from their touch device. Moreover, you want to notify the user by playing a notification sound as soon as a new order arrives in the system. This can be achieved by using the audio component which is provided by Sencha Touch and in this recipe. We will see how to use the audio component to play a sound.

Getting ready

Make sure that you have set up your development environment by following the recipes outlined in *Chapter 1*.

How to do it...

Carry out the following steps:

1. Create and open a new file named `ch07_02.js` and paste the following code into it:

```
Ext.setup({
    onReady: function() {
  var pnl = new Ext.Panel({
     fullscreen: true,
     items: [
         {
            id: 'audio-pnl',
            xtype: 'audio',
            url  : "ch07/here-it-is.mp3"
         }
     ],
     dockedItems: [{
                    xtype: 'toolbar',
                    dock: 'bottom',
                    items: [
                      {
                        text: 'Resume',
                        ui: 'confirm',
                        handler: function() {
                          var audioPnl = Ext.getCmp('audio-pnl');
                          audioPnl.play();
                        }
                      },
                      {
                        text: 'Stop',
```

```
                    handler: function() {
                      var audioPnl = Ext.getCmp('audio-pnl');
                      audioPnl.pause();
                    }
                  }
                ]
              }],
        listeners: {
          afterrender: function() {
            var audioPnl = Ext.getCmp('audio-pnl');
            audioPnl.play();
          }
        }
    });


      }
    });
```

2. Save your MP3 file inside the `ch07` folder and update the `url` property based on the MP3 file name.

3. Update the `index.html` file.

4. Deploy and access it from the browser or the device of your choice. You should see the following screen when it is run:

How it works...

The preceding code creates an audio component using `xtype: 'audio'` and the important property—`url`—is set to the path of the MP3 file that needs to be played. This, internally, uses the HTML5 audio field. By default, the audio component does not play the MP3 file. In order to get that working, we registered a handler for the `afterrender` event on the container panel and called the `play` method, explicitly, on the audio component.

Additionally, we created a docked toolbar with **Resume** and **Stop** buttons to play and stop the audio.

 Recommended file types are Uncompressed WAV and AIF audio, MP3 audio, and AAC-LC or HE-AAC audio.

See also

The recipe named *Setting up the browser-based development environment* in *Chapter 1*

Working with videos

In this recipe, we will look at the video component to see how to use it to add the video playing capability to our application.

Getting ready

Make sure that you have set up your development environment by following the recipes outlined in *Chapter 1*.

How to do it...

Carry out the following steps:

1. Create and open a new file named `ch07_03.js` and paste the following code in it:

```
Ext.setup({
    onReady: function() {
var pnl = new Ext.Panel({
    fullscreen: true,
    items: [
        {
            xtype    : 'video',
            id       : 'video-pnl',
```

```
                enableControls: false,
                x          : 600,
                y          : 300,
                width      : 300,
                height     : 250,
                url        : "ch07/space.mp4",
                posterUrl: "ch07/Screenshot.png"
            }
        ],
        dockedItems: [{
                    xtype: 'toolbar',
                    dock: 'bottom',
                    items: [
                        {
                          text: 'Resume',
                          ui: 'confirm',
                          handler: function() {
                            var videoPnl = Ext.getCmp('video-pnl');
                            videoPnl.play();
                          }
                        },
                        {
                          text: 'Stop',
                          handler: function() {
                            var videoPnl = Ext.getCmp('video-pnl');
                            videoPnl.pause();
                          }
                        }
                    ]
                }]
    });

        }
});
```

2. Save your MP4 file inside the ch07 folder and update the url property based on the MP4 file name.

3. Update index.html file.

4. Deploy and access it from the browser or the device of your choice and you should see the following screen:

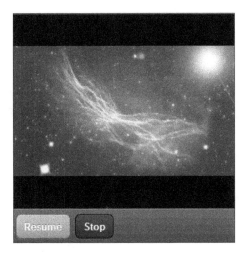

How it works...

The preceding code creates a video component using `xtype: 'video'` and the important property—`url`—is set to the path of the MP4 file that needs to be played. This, internally, uses the HTML5 video field.

Additionally, we create a docked toolbar with **Resume** and **Stop** buttons to play and stop the video.

`enableControls` allows us to control whether the control panel (with **Play/Pause** button, slider and sound buttons) should be displayed or not. As in our case, we are playing and pausing the video on a click of the toolbar buttons—**Resume** and **Stop**—we have set the property to `false`. By default, the controls are enabled. When the controls are enabled, we shall see the control as shown in the following screenshot:

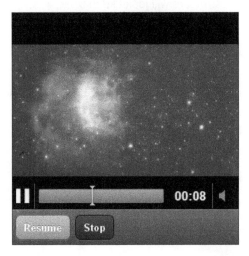

The recipe named *Setting up the browser-based development environment* in *Chapter 1*

Adding the chart support to your app

Data presentation is a key to decision making. While the tabular data can provide lot of details about a certain topic, the visual presentation can help us take quick decisions, especially when we have to compare the progression or regression of the data belonging to different categories. Sencha Touch comes with and add-on for charts. However, before we can start using them, we will have to set up our development environment with the chart support. In this recipe, we will go through the steps to download, install, and configure our project for Sencha Touch Charts.

Getting ready

Make sure that you have set up your development environment by following the recipes outlined in *Chapter 1*.

Download the Sencha Touch Charts framework from the Sencha website (http://www.sencha.com/products/charts/download/). We will be using the 1.0 version of the chart framework.

How to do it...

Carry out the following steps:

1. Extract the downloaded chart package into a temporary folder of your choice. Once extracted, the folder structure will look like this:

Name	Date modified	Type	Size
docs	02-08-2011 01:14 ...	File folder	
examples	02-08-2011 01:15 ...	File folder	
jsbuilder	02-08-2011 01:15 ...	File folder	
pkgs	02-08-2011 01:15 ...	File folder	
resources	02-08-2011 01:15 ...	File folder	
src	02-08-2011 01:15 ...	File folder	
build-touch-charts.bat	21-07-2011 09:55 ...	Windows Batch File	1 KB
build-touch-charts.sh	21-07-2011 09:55 ...	SH File	1 KB
fashion.exe	21-07-2011 09:55 ...	Application	909 KB
fashion_macosx	21-07-2011 09:55 ...	File	4,636 KB
generate-chart-themes.bat	21-07-2011 09:55 ...	Windows Batch File	1 KB
generate-chart-themes.sh	21-07-2011 09:55 ...	SH File	1 KB
index.html	21-07-2011 09:55 ...	HTML File	6 KB
license.inc	21-07-2011 09:55 ...	INC File	1 KB
license.txt	21-07-2011 09:55 ...	Text Document	10 KB
release-notes.html	21-07-2011 09:55 ...	HTML File	3 KB
sencha-touch.js	21-07-2011 09:55 ...	JS File	366 KB
sencha-touch-debug.js	21-07-2011 09:55 ...	JS File	1,431 KB
touch-charts.js	21-07-2011 09:55 ...	JS File	193 KB
touch-charts.jsb3	21-07-2011 09:55 ...	JSB3 File	7 KB
touch-charts-debug.js	21-07-2011 09:55 ...	JS File	674 KB

2. Create a `touch-charts` folder in your project's `assets/www` folder and copy the files from the extracted folder, as shown in the following screenshot. Refresh your project in Eclipse:

3. Update the `index.html` file with the following content:

```
<!DOCTYPE HTML>
<html>
  <head>
  <title>Yapps! - Your daily applications!</title>
  <link rel="stylesheet" href="touch-charts/resources/css/sencha-
    touch.css" type="text/css">
  <link rel="stylesheet" href="touch-charts/resources/css/touch-
    charts.css" type="text/css">
  <script type="text/javascript" charset="utf-8" src="phonegap-
    1.0.0.js"></script>
  <script type="text/javascript" charset="utf-8" src="touch-
    charts/sencha-touch-debug.js"></script>
  <script type="text/javascript" charset="utf-8" src="touch-
    charts/touch-charts-debug.js"></script>
  </head>
  <body></body>
</html>
```

How it works...

In step 2, we copied only the files and folders which are required to have the Sencha Touch framework along with the chart support. We cannot use the Sencha Touch framework files from the `assets/www/sencha-touch` folder as they have been modified for the charts support. Moreover, due to that, we updated the `index.html` file to have the right set of framework-related JS and CSS files included.

```
<link rel="stylesheet" href="touch-charts/resources/css/touch-
  charts.css" type="text/css">
```

The preceding line contains the chart-specific styles, for example, to style the legends and hence we included it in our `index.html` file.

See also

▶ The recipe named *Setting up the Android-based development environment* in *Chapter 1*

▶ The recipe named *Setting up the iOS-based development environment* in *Chapter 1*

▶ The recipe named *Setting up the Blackberry-based development environment* in *Chapter 1*

▶ The recipe named *Setting up the browser-based development environment* in *Chapter 1*

▶ The recipe named *Setting up the production environment* in *Chapter 1*

Working with an area chart

In this recipe, we will learn about the area chart provided by Sencha Touch. This creates a stacked area chart and is useful in displaying multiple aggregated layers of information.

Getting ready

Make sure that you have set up your development environment by following the recipes outlined in *Chapter 1*.

In all the chart-related recipes, we will be using the following store definition to feed the data to our charts:

```
var store = new Ext.data.JsonStore({
  fields: ['name', 'data1', 'data2', 'data3', 'data4', 'data5'],
  data: [
    {'name':'House Rent', 'data1':10, 'data2':12, 'data3':14,
      'data4':8, 'data5':13},
    {'name':'Books', 'data1':7, 'data2':8, 'data3':16, 'data4':10,
      'data5':3},
    {'name':'Petrol', 'data1':5, 'data2':2, 'data3':14, 'data4':12,
      'data5':7},
    {'name':'Grocery', 'data1':2, 'data2':14, 'data3':6, 'data4':1,
      'data5':23},
    {'name':'Loans & Deposits', 'data1':27, 'data2':38, 'data3':36,
      'data4':13, 'data5':33}
  ]
});
```

How to do it...

Carry out the following steps:

1. Create and open a new file named `ch07_04.js` and paste the following code into it:

```
Ext.setup({
    onReady: function() {
    var store = new Ext.data.JsonStore(...); //defined above

    var chart = new Ext.chart.Chart({
      fullscreen: true,
      width: 500,
      height: 300,
      store: store,
      axes: [{
```

```
            type: 'Numeric',
            position: 'left',
            fields: ['data1', 'data2', 'data3', 'data4', 'data5'],
            title: 'Sample Values',
            grid: {
              odd: {
                opacity: 1,
                fill: '#ddd',
                stroke: '#bbb',
                'stroke-width': 1
              }
            },
            minimum: 0

          },
          {
            type: 'Category',
            position: 'bottom',
            fields: ['name'],
            title: 'Sample Metrics',
            grid: true,
            label: {
              rotate: {
                degrees: 315
              }
            }
          }],
          series: [{
            type: 'area',
            highlight: false,
            axis: 'left',
            xField: 'name',
            yField: ['data1', 'data2', 'data3', 'data4', 'data5'],
            style: {
                opacity: 0.93
            }
          }]
        });

        }
    });
```

2. Update the `index.html` file.

3. Deploy and access it from the browser or the device of your choice. You will see the following screen:

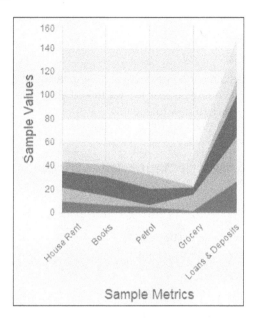

How it works...

The preceding code creates the high-level `Ext.chart.Chart` instance, which provides the capability to visualize the data. This object accepts four important properties: `store`, `legend`, `axes`, and `series`. The `store` property binds a data source to the chart, so that the chart can be updated dynamically. The `legend` property displays a list of legend items, each of them related to a series being rendered. This is optional. The `axes` property contains the definition of the Cartesian axis and the field from the data set will be used to render the x and y axis. The `series` property indicates the kind of chart that needs to be rendered using the data stored in the `store` and the `axes` definition.

In the code, we have defined two axes: one of type `Numeric` and other of type `Category`. Each entry in `axes` is represented by `Ext.chart.axis.Axis` class. `grid:true` tells that the grid line should be displayed for the axis. For the `Numeric` axis, we defined `grid` as a config object containing the information about how the odd rows in the grid should be rendered.

Another property that the `axes` supports is `label`, which allows us to provide the information about how the label should be displayed. In the preceding code, we have mentioned that the label should be displayed at an angle of 315 degree with respect to the axis.

Then, we added the series of type area to create the area chart. The `axis` property sets the position of the axes. `xField` and `yField` properties provide the mapping of the field in the data to the axis where they should be displayed.

There's more...

Having a legend in a chart is almost a necessity and Sencha Touch does support this in its chart functionality. In the preceding discussion, we talked about the optional property on the `Chart` object—`legend`. Let us see how to use it.

Showing legend

1. Add the `legend` config to the `Chart` object as follows:

```
legend: {
        field: 'name',
    position: {
        portrait: 'bottom',
        landscape: 'right'
    }
}
```

In the preceding code, we have defined a `legend` metadata where the name field from the data set will be used to generate the legend. However, if the view is in portrait mode, the legend will be displayed at the bottom of the chart, whereas in case of landscape mode, the legend will be displayed on the right-hand side of the chart.

2. Set `showInLegend` property to `true` on the series

These changes to the code will ensure that the legend is generated for the chart as shown in the following screenshot:

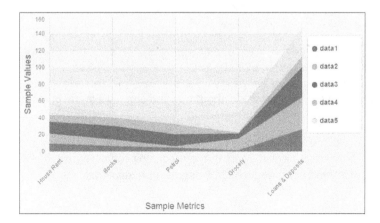

Changing the legend text

By default, the chart library uses the field name mentioned in `yField` on the `series`. In order to have a different legend text, add the `title` config to the `series` as follows:

```
title:['Sample 1','Sample 2','Sample 3','Sample 4','Sample 5'],
```

In the preceding code, we have defined a title for each sample data, which the chart library will use to show the legend text, as shown in the following screenshot:

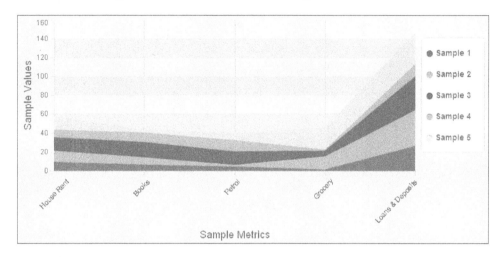

See also

▸ The recipe named *Setting up browser-based development environment* in *Chapter 1*
▸ The recipe named *Working with Store* in *Chapter 5*

Generating a bar chart

Bar chart is another series which can be used to help the user visualize and compare the data. In this recipe, we will see how to use the bar series to get a bar chart generated.

Getting ready

Make sure that you have set up your development environment by following the recipes outlined in *Chapter 1*.

How to do it...

Carry out the following steps:

1. Create and open a new file named ch07_05.js and paste the following code into it:

```
Ext.setup({
    onReady: function() {
    var store = new Ext.data.JsonStore(...); //defined in Area
Chart recipe

        var chart = new Ext.chart.Chart({
            fullscreen: true,
            width: 500,
          height: 300;
          animate: true,
          store: store,
          axes: [{
              type: 'Numeric',
              position: 'bottom',
              fields: ['data1'],
              title: 'Sample Values',
              grid: true,
              minimum: 0
          }, {
              type: 'Category',
              position: 'left',
              fields: ['name'],
              title: 'Sample Metrics'
          }],
          series: [{
              type: 'bar',
              axis: 'bottom',
              highlight: true,
              label: {
                  field: 'data1',
                  orientation: 'horizontal',
                  color: '#333',
                  'text-anchor': 'middle'
              },
              xField: 'name',
              yField: ['data1']
          }]
    });

    }
});
```

2. Update the `index.html` file.

3. Deploy and access it from the browser or the device of your choice. You will see the following screen:

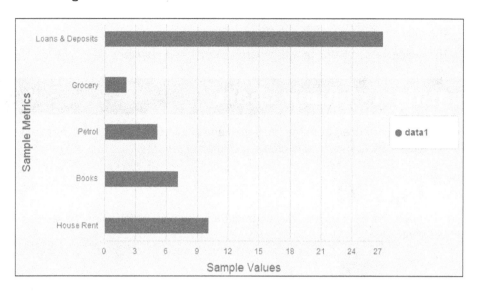

How it works...

In the preceding code, we created an instance of the `Chart` object with `axes` and `series` information. In `series`, we set `type` to `bar` to get the bar chart generated from the data set.

There's more...

The default spacing between the bars is derived by the bar series. However, if there is a need to increase or decrease the gap between them, here is the way to do that.

Changing the spacing between the bars

On the bar series, there is a property named `gutter` which accepts numeric values in pixels. The value set to `gutter` is used as the gap between two bars. For example, if `gutter:200` is set on the series configuration, then the spacing between two bars will be 200 pixels.

See also

▸ The recipe named *Setting up the browser-based development* environment in *Chapter 1*

▸ The recipe named *Working with Store* in *Chapter 5*

▸ The recipe named *Working with an area chart* in this chapter

Creating a column chart

The column chart is extended from the bar series and displays the chart in the form of vertical bars. In this recipe, we will see how to create a column chart.

Getting ready

Make sure that you have set up your development environment by following the recipes outlined in *Chapter 1*.

How to do it...

Carry out the following steps:

1. Create and open a new file named `ch07_06.js` and paste the following code into it:

```
Ext.setup({
    onReady: function() {
     var store = new Ext.data.JsonStore(...);   //defined in Area
       Chart recipe

     var chart = new Ext.chart.Chart({
       fullscreen: true,
       width: 500,
       height: 300,
       animate: true,
       store: store,
       axes: [{
         type: 'Numeric',
         position: 'bottom',
         fields: ['data1'],
         title: 'Sample Values',
         grid: true,
         minimum: 0
         }, {
             type: 'Category',
```

```
                position: 'left',
                fields: ['name'],
                title: 'Sample Metrics'
        }],
        series: [{
          type: 'column',
          axis: 'left',
          highlight: true,
          label: {
            'text-anchor': 'middle',
            field: ['data1'],
            orientation: 'vertical',
            color: '#333'
          },
            xField: 'name',
            yField: ['data1']
        }]
    });

    }
});
```

2. Update the `index.html` file.

3. Deploy and access it from the browser or the device of your choice. You will see the following screen:

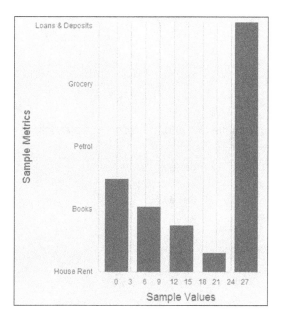

How it works...

The preceding code creates an instance of a `Chart` with `axes` and a `series` of `type` `column`.

See also

▶ The recipe named *Setting up the browser-based development* environment in *Chapter 1*

▶ The recipe named *Working with Store* in *Chapter 5*

▶ The recipe named *Working with an area chart* in this chapter

Showing a group of bars and columns

Our data set contains `data1`, `data2`, `data3`, `data4`, and `data5` fields, besides the `name` field. Suppose, for every month for your monthly expenses, `data1` represents the actual expense whereas `data2` represents the estimated expense and we want to see the visuals for both the values being presented for each of the expense categories, that is, we need to show a group of bars for each category. In the bar and column charts, Sencha Touch supports showing a group of bars in the place of a single bar. This recipe will show how to do that.

Getting ready

Make sure that you have set up your development environment by following the recipes outlined in *Chapter 1*.

How to do it...

Carry out the following steps:

1. Edit the `ch07_06.js` file and add the properties highlighted in bold, as follows:

```
axes: [{
            type: 'Numeric',
            position: 'bottom',
            fields: ['data1', 'data2'],
            title: 'Sample Values',
            grid: true,
            minimum: 0
        }, {
          type: 'Category',
          position: 'left',
```

```
        fields: ['name'],
        title: 'Sample Metrics'
      }],
      series: [{
        type: 'column',
        axis: 'left',
        highlight: true,
        label: {
          display: 'insideEnd',
          'text-anchor': 'middle',
          field: ['data1', 'data2'],
          orientation: 'vertical',
          color: '#333'
        },
        xField: 'name',
        yField: ['data1', 'data2']
      }],
```

2. Deploy and access the application from the browser or the device of your choice. You will see the following screen:

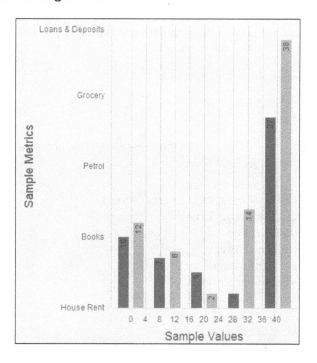

▶ The recipe named *Setting up the browser-based development* environment in *Chapter 1*

▶ The recipe named *Working with Store* in *Chapter 5*

▶ The recipe named *Working with an area chart* in this chapter

▶ The recipe named *Creating a column chart* in this chapter

Switching between stacked and grouped orientation

In previous recipes, we saw how to get grouped bars in a bar or a column chart. The Sencha Touch Chart framework provides functionality where using one of the tap events, the grouped bars can be converted into stacked bars and vice versa. This recipe will show how to use that functionality.

Getting ready

Make sure that you have set up your development environment by following the recipes outlined in *Chapter 1*.

How to do it...

Carry our the following steps:

1. Edit the ch07_06.js file and add the interactions properties, highlighted in bold, to the chart object as follows:

```
var chart = new Ext.chart.Chart({
    fullscreen: true,
    width: 500,
    height: 300,
    animate: true,
    store: store,
    axes: [................],
        series: [.............],
    interactions: [{
      type: 'togglestacked'
    }]
});
```

2. Save the change and access the application from the browser or the device of your choice.

3. Touch the bar and swipe. You will see the bars stacked as shown in the below screenshot:

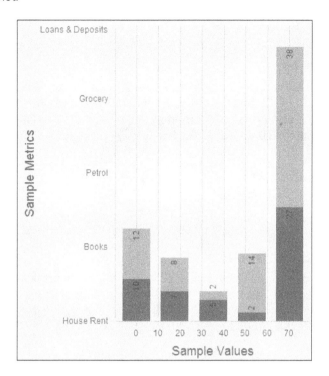

How it works...

In the preceding code, we added an `interactions` array with one a member of type `togglestacked` which provides us the functionality of stacking the bars.

The `Chart` component in Sencha Touch provides a support for interactions and gestures, which help us, build interactive charts. The framework provides a list of interactions which can be used for different types of series. Each interaction is driven by a gesture, such as, tap, doubletap, swipe, pinch, and so on. By default, every interaction is mapped to a specific event. For example, in our case, the `togglestacked` is mapped to `swipe`.

This interaction can be used on the bar as well as column series.

There's more...

First thing, in an application, we may want to change the default swipe gesture which is used for `togglestacked` to, say, `doubletap`. In addition, during the interaction we might have changed the state of the chart, which we may want to reset it back to its original state. Let us see how to achieve these requirements.

Changing gesture

Besides the `type` property, an item in the `interactions` array contains an additional property named `gesture`. Setting this to the event name, which will fire up the interaction, will change the default gesture value. For example, to invoke the `togglestacked` interaction on `doubletap`, the interaction will look like this:

```
{
type: 'togglestacked',
    gesture: 'doubletap'
}
```

Resetting the chart state

In order to reset the chart state to its original state, Sencha Touch provides an interaction of `type` `reset`. When used, the chart is reset when the user doubletaps on the empty part of the chart. The following code snippet shows how to add the reset behavior to a chart by adding the following to the `interactions` array:

```
{
   type: 'reset'
}
```

See also

- ▸ The recipe named *Setting up the browser-based development* environment in *Chapter 1*
- ▸ The recipe named *Working with Store* in *Chapter 5*
- ▸ The recipe named *Working with an area chart* in this chapter
- ▸ The recipe named *Creating a column chart* in this chapter

Highlighting and displaying an item detail

The next level of interaction is that when the user clicks on a chart item, we may want to highlight that item and show the item detail corresponding to it. In this recipe, we will see how to achieve this.

Getting ready

Make sure that you have set up your development environment by following the recipes outlined in *Chapter 1*.

How to do it...

Carry out the following steps:

1. Edit the `ch07_06.js` file.
2. Add the following interactions to the chart's `interactions` array:

```
{
    type: 'iteminfo',
    gesture: 'taphold',
    listeners: {
      show: function(me, item, panel) {
        panel.update(item.value[0] + " : " + item.value[1]);
      }
    }
},
{
    type: 'itemhighlight'
}
```

3. Save the change.
4. Deploy and access it from the browser or the device of your choice.
5. Single tap on a bar, this will highlight the bar.

6. Tap on the bar and hold it for a while. You will see a pop-up showing the item detail as shown in the following screenshot:

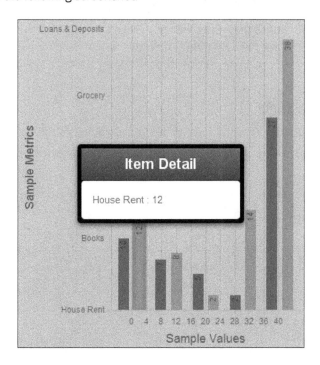

How it works...

The code uses the two of the in-built interactions: `itemhighlight` and `iteminfo`. The default handler of the `iteminfo` interaction shows a pop-up panel with **Item Detail** as the title. This panel is passed to the `show` event handler as the third argument which we updated with the selected item detail.

See also

▸ The recipe named *Setting up the browser-based development* environment in *Chapter 1*

▸ The recipe named *Working with Store* in *Chapter 5*

▸ The recipe named *Working with an area chart* in this chapter

▸ The recipe named *Creating a column chart* in this chapter

Creating a gauge chart

Gauge charts are used to show the progress in a certain variable. In this recipe, we will walk through the steps to create a gauge chart.

Getting ready

Make sure that you have set up your development environment by following the recipes outlined in *Chapter 1*.

How to do it...

Carry out the following steps:

1. Create and open a new file named `ch07_07.js` and paste the following code into it:

```
Ext.setup({
    onReady: function() {
      var store = new Ext.data.JsonStore(...); //defined in the
        Area Chart recipe

      var chart = new Ext.chart.Chart({
          fullscreen: true,
          width: 500,
          height: 300,
          animate: true,
          store: store,
          axes: [{
            type: 'gauge',
            position: 'gauge',
            minimum: 0,
            maximum: 100,
            steps: 10
          }],
          series: [{
              type: 'gauge',
              angleField: 'data1',
              colorSet: ['#F49D10', '#123456']
          }],
            interactions: [{
                type: 'rotate'
          }]
      });
    }
});
```

2. Update the `index.html` file.

3. Deploy and access it from the browser. You may also run it using the emulator. You will then see the following screen:

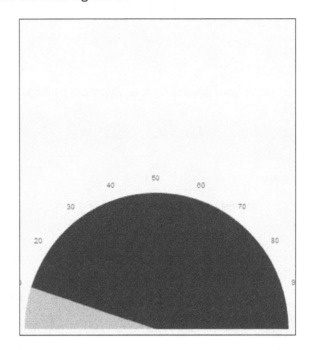

How it works...

The preceding code creates a `Chart` object with series of `type` gauge. The gauge chart requires a special `axis` named gauge. Therefore, we set up the `axes` detail using the gauge type, the starting number, the ending number, and the steps to be displayed along the circumference of the semicircle. `position` is set to gauge in the `Ext.axis.chart.Gauge`, by default, but we have to set it again to get around an issue in the framework.

In `series`, after the `type` property, the next important property is `angleField`, which contains the field name of the record that is used for the gauge angles. The value must be a positive real number. `colorSet` is used to specify colors that will be used to render the sections/pies of the gauge chart.

Lastly, we configured the rotation interaction on the gauge chart.

There are some more useful properties of the gauge chart which are worth discussing.

Showing a needle

On a gauge, sometime we may want to see a needle to show something like a dial chart. This can be achieved by setting the `needle` property to `true` on the gauge series.

The donut effect

The donut effect can be created by setting the `donut` property on the gauge series to a value which is used as the radius of the inner circle. For example, this is how the gauge will look if we set the donut to 50:

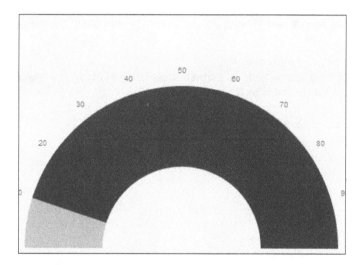

See also

- ▶ The recipe named *Setting up the browser-based development* environment in *Chapter 1*
- ▶ The recipe named *Working with Store* in *Chapter 5*
- ▶ The recipe named *Working with an area chart* in this chapter

Creating a line chart

This recipe is all about creating a line chart by using the Sencha Touch Chart library.

Getting ready

Make sure that you have set up your development environment by following the recipes outlined in *Chapter 1*.

How to do it...

Carry out the following steps:

1. Create and open a new file named `ch07_08.js` and paste the following code into it:

```
Ext.setup({
    onReady: function() {
        var store = new Ext.data.JsonStore(...);  //defined in
            the Area Chart recipe

        var chart = new Ext.chart.Chart({
            fullscreen: true,
            width: 500,
            height: 300,
            animate: true,
            store: store,
            axes: [{
                type: 'Numeric',
                position: 'bottom',
                fields: ['data1'],
                title: 'Sample Values',
                grid: true,
                minimum: 0
            }, {
                type: 'Category',
                position: 'left',
                fields: ['name'],
                title: 'Sample Metrics'
            }],
            series: [{
                type: 'line',
                highlight: {
                    size: 7,
```

```
            radius: 7
        },
          axis: 'left',
          xField: 'name',
          yField: 'data1'
      }, {
          type: 'line',
          highlight: {
            size: 7,
            radius: 7
          },
          axis: 'left',
          xField: 'name',
          yField: 'data3'
      }],
        interactions: [{
          type: 'reset'
        },
        {
          type: 'panzoom',
          axes: {
            left: {}
          }
        },
        {
          type: 'iteminfo',
          gesture: 'taphold'
        },
        {
          type: 'itemcompare'
        }]
    });

    }
  });
```

2. Update the index.html file.

3. Deploy and access it from the browser. You may also run it using the emulator. You will then see the following screen:

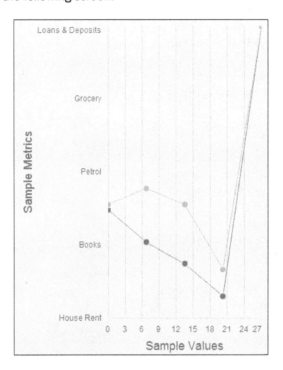

How it works...

The preceding code creates a `Chart` object with a `line type` series various interactions. In each of the `series`, the `highlight` config object defines the configuration which is used to highlight the line and the nodes when the user taps on a particular line series. It will show the circle with a 7-pixel radius.

There's more...

Let us look at some of the additional useful properties of the line chart.

Filling the area

In order to fill the area under a line series, we will set the `fill` property to `true` on the particular line series. For example, if we want to show the color under our first line series, then we will set the property on it as follows:

```
series: [{
        type: 'line',
        fill: true,
```

```
        highlight: {
          size: 7,
          radius: 7
          ...
        }
      }]
```

Smooth curves

By default, the curve will have edges. However, if we want smooth curves such as the ones drawn by the Bezier or B-Spline curves, then we must set the property `smooth` to `true` on the desired line series. The following code snippet shows how to set this property:

```
series: [{
        type: 'line',
        fill: true,
        smooth: true,
        highlight: {
          size: 7,
          radius: 7
          ...
        }
      }]
```

Once these properties are set, the chart will look similar to the one shown in the following screenshot:

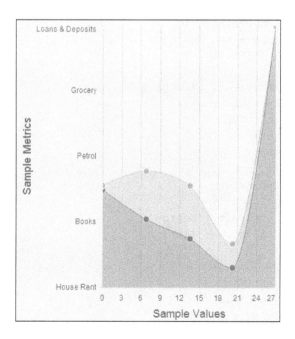

See also

▶ The recipe named *Setting up the browser-based development* environment in *Chapter 1*

▶ The recipe named *Working with Store* in *Chapter 5*

▶ The recipe named *Working with an area chart* in this chapter

Creating a pie chart

This recipe shows how to create a pie chart and work with some interesting features offered by the framework.

Getting ready

Make sure that you have set up your development environment by following the recipes outlined in *Chapter 1*.

How to do it...

Carry out the following steps:

1. Create and open a new file named `ch07_09.js` and paste the following code into it:

```
Ext.setup({
    onReady: function() {
      var store = new Ext.data.JsonStore(...);  //defined in the
        Area Chart recipe

      var chart = new Ext.chart.Chart({
        fullscreen: true,
        width: 500,
        height: 300,
        animate: true,
        store: store,
        legend: {
          position: {
            portrait: 'bottom',
            landscape: 'left'
          }
        },
        series: [{
          type: 'pie',
          angleField: 'data1',
```

```
            showInLegend: true,
            label: {
              field: 'name',
              display: 'rotate',
              font: '18px Arial'
            }
          }]
      });


      }
    });
```

2. Update the `index.html` file.

3. Deploy and access it from the browser. You may also run it using the emulator. You will then see the following screen:

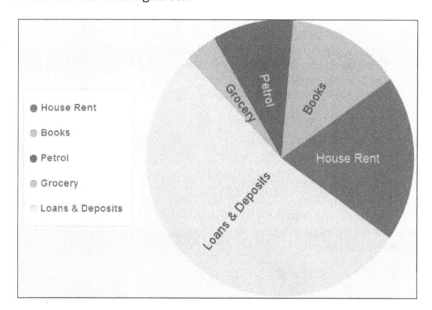

How it works...

The preceding code creates a `Chart` object with `series` of type `pie`. The `angleField` is the record field which is used to calculate the angle. `showInLegend` is set to `true` to generate the legend using the `legend` configuration specified within the chart.

The `label` config contains the information about how the label for each pie will be generated. `field` is the record field name whose value should be used as the label text. Setting `contrast` to `true` will ensure that the label is displayed in a black or white color based on the pie color, so that it is readable. `font` contains the font information that should be used for the label text.

There's more...

Let us look at some of the other properties which might be of our interest.

The donut effect

Similar to the gauge chart, the donut effect can be created by setting the `donut` property on the pie series with a positive numeric value.

Pie length derived from the data

In some presentation use cases, we may have to display the pie with its radius derived from one of the data fields. If this is the case, we can do this by setting the `lengthField` property on the pie series. The value assigned to this property must be a record field. The following code shows how to use this property:

```
series: [{
            type: 'pie',
            angleField: 'data1',
            lengthField: 'data1',
    ...
}]
```

The following screenshot, the first one where the pie length is derived from data and the second one is where it shows the donut, shows how the pie chart will look like after these additional properties are set:

See also

▶ The recipe named *Setting up the browser-based development* environment in *Chapter 1*

▶ The recipe named *Working with Store* in *Chapter 5*

▶ The recipe named *Working with an area chart* in this chapter

Rotating the pies

Coming to the interactions with the pie chart, rotation is one of them, which allows the user to rotate the pie chart to view a pie at a particular position. In this recipe, we will learn how to achieve this.

Getting ready

Make sure that you have set up your development environment by following the recipes outlined in *Chapter 1*.

How to do it...

Carry out the following steps:

1. Edit the ch07_09.js file.
2. Add the following interaction item to it:

```
interactions: [{
  type: 'rotate'
}]
```

3. Save the changes.
4. Deploy and access the application from the browser. You may also run it using the emulator.
5. Use the single-finger or mouse drag, based on your device, around the center of the series. You will see the pie chart rotating.

How it works...

This is taken care of by the default rotate interaction of the Sencha Touch Chart framework.

See also

▶ The recipe named *Setting up the browser-based development* environment in *Chapter 1*

▶ The recipe named *Working with Store* in *Chapter 5*

▶ The recipe named *Working with an area chart* in this chapter

▶ The recipe named *Creating a pie chart* in this chapter

Grouping the pies

Another useful feature is while you are analyzing your data using the pie chart, you may want to group multiple pies and get additional information; for example, what is the cumulative expense for the House Rent and Petrol. In this recipe, we will see how to put this in place.

Getting ready

Make sure that you have set up your development environment by following the recipes outlined in *Chapter 1*.

How to do it...

Carry out the following steps:

1. Edit the `ch07_09.js` file.
2. Add the following interaction item into it:

```
interactions: [{
  type: 'piegrouping',
  listeners: {
    selectionchange: function(interaction, selectedItems) {
      var msg = selectedItems.length + ' items
          grouped!\nItems are: ';
      Ext.each(selectedItems, function(item, idx, allItems) {
        msg += ' - ' + item.storeItem.data.name;
      });

      Ext.Msg.alert('INFO', msg);
    }
  }
}]
```

3. Save the changes.

4. Deploy and access the application from the browser. You may also run it using the emulator.

5. Tap a particular pie. This will show a handle which we can drag around other pies to add/remove the slices to/from the selection group, and once grouped it will show an alert message indicating the items, which have been grouped, as shown in the following screenshot:

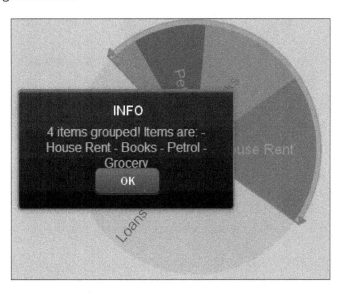

How it works...

This is taken care of by the default `piegrouping` interaction of the Sencha Touch Chart framework. Upon grouping of the pies, the interaction fires the `selectionchange` event which we have handled to show the selected items.

See also

- ▶ The recipe named *Setting up the browser-based development* environment in *Chapter 1*
- ▶ The recipe named *Working with Store* in *Chapter 5*
- ▶ The recipe named *Working with an area chart* in this chapter
- ▶ The recipe named *Creating a pie chart* in this chapter

Highlighting a pie

One fascinating feature the pie chart supports is highlighting a pie and when it is selected. It actually stands out distinctly from other pies. In this recipe, we will see how to make use of this feature.

Getting ready

Make sure that you have set up your development environment by following the recipes outlined in *Chapter 1*.

1. Edit the ch07_09.js file.

2. Add the following interaction item to it:

    ```
    interactions: [{
      type: 'itemhighlight'
    }]
    ```

3. Save the changes.

4. Deploy and access the application from the browser. You may also run it using the emulator.

5. Tap a particular pie. This will show the pie highlighted and stand out from the rest of the chart, as shown in the following screenshot:

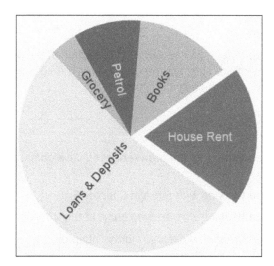

How it works...

This is taken care of by the default `itemhighlight` interaction on the pie series of the Sencha Touch Chart framework.

See also

▸ The recipe named *Setting up the browser-based development* environment in *Chapter 1*

▸ The recipe named *Working with Store* in *Chapter 5*

▸ The recipe named *Working with an area chart* in this chapter

▸ The recipe named *Creating a pie chart* in this chapter

Using a radar chart

A radar chart is a useful visualization technique for comparing different quantitative values for a constrained number of categories, and this recipe will show us how to create a radar chart.

Getting ready

Make sure that you have set up your development environment by following the recipes outlined in *Chapter 1*.

How to do it...

Carry out the following steps:

1. Create and open a new file named `ch07_10.js` and paste the following code into it:

```
Ext.setup({
    onReady: function() {
    var store = new Ext.data.JsonStore(...);   //defined in Area
      Chart recipe

      var chart = new Ext.chart.Chart({
        fullscreen: true,
        width: 500,
        height: 300,
        animate: true,
        store: store,
        axes: [{
            type: 'Radial',
```

```
            position: 'radial',
            label: {
                display: true
            }
        }],
        legend: {
            field: 'name',
        position: {
            portrait: 'bottom',
            landscape: 'right'
        }
        },
        series: [{
            type: 'radar',
            xField: 'name',
            yField: 'data3',
            showInLegend: true,
            showMarkers: true,
            style: {
                'stroke-width': 2,
                fill: '#abcdef',
                opacity: 0.4
            }
        },{
            type: 'radar',
            xField: 'name',
            yField: 'data2',
            showMarkers: true,
            showInLegend: true,
            style: {
                'stroke-width': 2,
                fill: '#5d5f4d',
                opacity: 0.4
            }
        },{
            type: 'radar',
            xField: 'name',
            yField: 'data5',
            showMarkers: true,
            showInLegend: true,
            style: {
                'stroke-width': 4,
                fill: '#ddd',
                opacity: 0.4
```

```
                }
            }]
        });


            }
        });
```

2. Update the `index.html` file.

3. Deploy and access it from the browser. You may also run it using the emulator. You will then see the following screen:

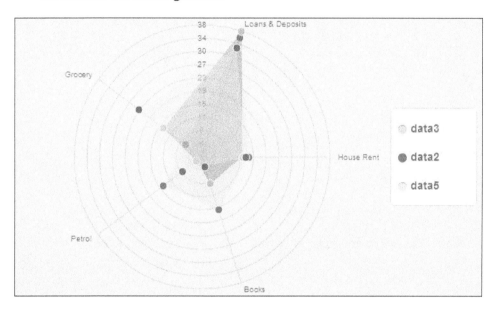

How it works...

The preceding code creates a `Chart` object with a `series` of type `radar`. `xField` and `yField` are the record field names that are used to render the radar. `style` is used to style each of the series by using the properties defined in it. In the `style` config object, we set the `fill` color and the transparency level. `showInLegend` is set to `true` to add the series data to the legend.

There's more...

By default, the series uses `circle` as the marker. If we want to use a different one, following is how we will do it.

Using a different marker

The kind of marker to be used is derived from the `type` property of the `markerConfig` object. The following code, in bold, shows the usage of `cross` as the marker for one of the series:

```
{
        type: 'radar',
        xField: 'name',
        yField: 'data5',
        showMarkers: true,
        showInLegend: true,
        markerConfig: {
          type: 'cross',
            size: 5
        },
        style: {
  ...}
  }
```

Once set, the following screenshot shows what the new marker will look like:

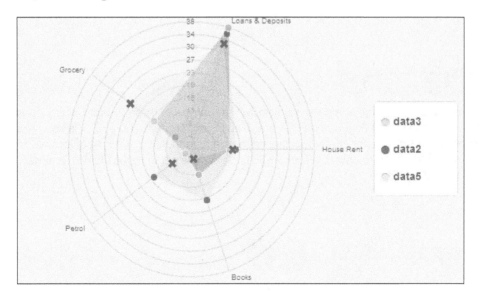

See also

▸ The recipe named *Setting up the browser-based development* environment in *Chapter 1*

▸ The recipe named *Working with Store* in *Chapter 5*

▸ The recipe named *Working with an area chart* in this chapter

Using a scatter chart

The scatter plot is useful when trying to display more than two variables in the same visualization. This recipe will show us how to work with a scatter chart.

Getting ready

Make sure that you have set up your development environment by following the recipes outlined in *Chapter 1*.

How to do it...

Carry out the following steps:

1. Create and open a new file named `ch07_11.js` and paste the following code into it:

```
Ext.setup({
    onReady: function() {
      var store = new Ext.data.JsonStore(...);  //defined in
        the Area Chart recipe

      var chart = new Ext.chart.Chart({
          fullscreen: true,
        width: 500,
        height: 300,
        animate: true,
        store: store,
        axes: [{
            type: 'Numeric',
            position: 'bottom',
            fields: ['data1', 'data2', 'data3'],
            title: 'Sample Values',
            grid: true,
            minimum: 0
        }, {
            type: 'Category',
```

```
            position: 'left',
            fields: ['name'],
            title: 'Sample Metrics'
    }],
      legend: {
        field: 'name',
      position: {
        portrait: 'bottom',
        landscape: 'right'
      }
    },
    series: [{
        type: 'scatter',
        axis: 'left',
        xField: 'name',
        yField: 'data1'
    },{
        type: 'scatter',
        markerConfig: {
          type: 'plus',
            radius: 5,
            size: 5
        },
        axis: 'left',
        xField: 'name',
        yField: 'data2'
    }, {
        type: 'scatter',
        markerConfig: {
          type: 'cross',
            size: 5
        },
        axis: 'left',
        xField: 'name',
        yField: 'data3'
    }],
      interactions: [{
        type: 'reset'
      },
      {
        type: 'panzoom',
        axes: {
          left: {}
        }
```

```
            },
            {
              type: 'iteminfo',
              gesture: 'taphold'
            }]
        });

      }
    });
```

2. Update the `index.html` file.

3. Deploy and access it from the browser. You may also run it using the emulator. You will then see the following screen:

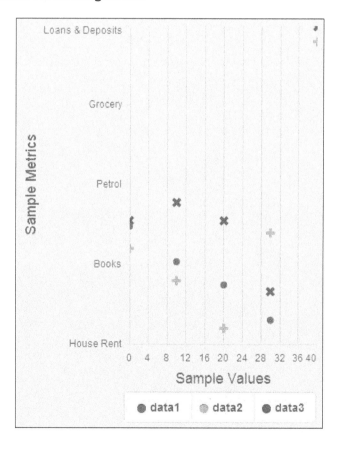

How it works...

The preceding code creates a `Chart` object with a `series` of `type scatter`. Each series contains `xField` and `yField` properties which are set to the record data fields. `markerConfig` contains the markers that need to be used for each of the scatter series.

In addition, there are three interactions added: `reset`, `panzoom`, and `iteminfo`. As there is no handler written for the show event in case of `iteminfo`, `taphold` will show a blank pop-up with the title **Item Detail**.

See also

▶   The recipe named *Setting up the browser-based development* environment in *Chapter 1*

▶   The recipe named *Working with Store* in *Chapter 5*

▶   The recipe named *Working with an area chart* in this chapter

8
Taking your Application Offline

In this chapter, we will cover:

- ▶ Detecting offline mode
- ▶ Storing your data offline
- ▶ Storing your images offline
- ▶ Application caching

Introduction

When it comes to building mobile applications, there is one special case that is different to the mobile application from today's desktop applications—**offline mode** or the **flight mode**. However, this offline mode has been there on desktop applications for some time, where we had intermittent or slow network connections. However, they are now more common to the mobile world. This mode means the mobile is not on the network and does not have access to the WLAN or GPRS data connection.

There are several cases where it is necessary for an application to have an offline presence. For example, imagine that you are field maintenance staff and you work in areas where there is no network coverage. However, you need to carry the list of customers, their orders, and the order details containing the list of products the customer has ordered, their quantity, prices, and so on. As field maintenance staff, you are expected to fulfill the order, collect the payment, and issue a receipt to customers. Moreover, in your company, the order is created in a centralized ERP system. In this case, it would be impossible to manage things electronically if the offline application to enable the field maintenance staff was not there. A typical offline application can help the maintenance staff to download the orders for a day on their mobile. This will enable them to update the order status locally on their mobile, create, and issue a receipt to the customer after the order is completed, come back to their office and sync up the updated orders and the receipts and other updates with the centralized system. I am sure there can be much more interesting scenarios where offline applications would be useful. The bottom line is that having an offline capability in our application makes a lot of sense and is a powerful feature to have in a mobile application.

A typical touch application consists of one or more JavaScript files, one or more CSS files and work with the data and images. Taking this application offline means all these things should be made available on the local device and should be stored in such a way that the absence of the network does not make any difference to the application. In this chapter, we will see how to take our application completely offline and learn how to model our application for online and offline mode support.

Detecting offline mode

The life of an offline application starts with identifying whether the device/browser is online or offline and, based on that, taking the appropriate action. In this recipe, we will see the different ways that we can identify whether the device or the browser is online or offline, which would help us make decisions in the subsequent recipes. We will start with using PhoneGap API to detect the mode and then later look at other alternatives.

We have already set up our project with PhoneGap support as part of the setup in *Chapter 1*. You may refer to `http://docs.phonegap.com` for more details on its APIs.

Getting ready

Make sure that you have set up your development environment by following the recipes outlined in *Chapter 1*.

Create a new folder named `ch08` in the same folder where we created the `ch01` and `ch02` folders. We will be using this new folder in which to keep the code.

How to do it...

Carry out the following steps:

1. Create and open a new file named `ch08_01.js` and paste the following code into it:

```
Ext.setup({
  onReady: function() {

    //phonegap way to detect connection
    var networkState = navigator.network.connection.type;

    var states = {};
    states[Connection.UNKNOWN]  = 'Unknown connection';
    states[Connection.ETHERNET] = 'Ethernet connection';
    states[Connection.WIFI]     = 'WiFi connection';
    states[Connection.CELL_2G]  = 'Cell 2G connection';
    states[Connection.CELL_3G]  = 'Cell 3G connection';
    states[Connection.CELL_4G]  = 'Cell 4G connection';
    states[Connection.NONE]     = 'No network connection';

    var str = (navigator.onLine ? 'ONLINE' : 'OFFLINE') + ' - ' +
      states[networkState];

    Ext.Msg.alert('INFO', str);
  }
});
```

2. Update the `index.html` file.

3. Deploy and access it from the device of your choice.

How it works...

`navigator.network.connection.type` gets the connection type from the `navigator` JavaScript object and is used to compare the network status values defined in the PhoneGap's `Connection` object to determine whether the device is online or offline. Additionally, the `Connection` object gives more information about the kind of network available in the online case. `Connection.NONE` indicates the offline mode of the device.

`navigator.onLine` allows us to check if the browser is in online or offline mode. This is different from the device online/offline mode. Many browsers would say they are online even if there is no network.

At the time of writing this chapter, the `Connection` API supports the following platforms: (a) iOS (b) Android (c) BlackBerry WebWorks (OS 5.0 and higher).

There's more...

The preceding code works well as long as we are using the compatible browsers which support the property on the `navigator` object and the PhoneGap APIs. However, using PhoneGap is not mandatory for creating Sencha Touch based applications. There is one more technique which we can use to identify the offline mode. Let's see how to use that technique.

Using aggressive timeout

In *Chapter 5, Dealing with Data and Data Sources*, we saw how to use stores and proxies to connect to the data sources and load the data. Proxy is configured on a model. To figure out if we are in online or offline mode, we can use the `timeout` property on the proxy and set a very small timeout period. If the connection fails, then the `exception` handler will take care of using the offline data for the application, as shown in the following code snippet:

```
proxy: {
  type: 'ajax',
  url : 'orders.json',
  reader: {
      type: 'json',
      root: 'orders',
      totalProperty: 'totalRecords',
      successProperty: 'success'
  },
  timeout: 2000,
  listeners: {
    exception:function (proxy, response, operation) {
      //we are offline
    }
  }
}
```

See also

▶ The recipe named *Setting up the Android-based development environment* in *Chapter 1*

▶ The recipe named *Setting up the iOS-based development environment* in *Chapter 1*

▶ The recipe named *Setting up the Blackberry-based development environment* in *Chapter 1*

▶ The recipe named *Setting up the browser-based development environment* in *Chapter 1*

▶ The recipe named *Setting up the production environment* in *Chapter 1*

▶ The recipe named *Loading data through AJAX using AjaxProxy* in *Chapter 5*

Storing your data offline

Any application has to deal with the data to provide a rich set of functionality. Moreover, when the application goes offline, the data which is required to work with that also needs to be available locally. In this recipe, we will look at how to take our data offline and use it in the application.

In this recipe, we have taken an example of an application which will download the list of orders and their details on the device and use it in the application to allow the user to look at the list of orders and their details.

Getting ready

Make sure that you have set up your development environment by following the recipes outlined in *Chapter 1*.

How to do it...

Carry out the following steps:

1. Create and open a new file named `ch08_02.js` and paste the following code into it:

```
Ext.setup({
    onReady: function() {

    var orderList, onlineStore, offlineStore;

    //OrderLine model representing a line item in an order
     Ext.regModel('OrderLine', {
        fields: ['id', 'product', 'description', 'orderedQty',
          'uom', 'price']
    });

    //Order model representing an order in the system
     Ext.regModel('Order', {
        fields: [
          'id',
          {name: 'orderNbr',  type: 'int', mapping: 'documentNo'},
          {name: 'description',   type: 'string'},
```

```
                {name: 'dateOrdered', type: 'string'},
                {name: 'customer', type: 'string'},
                {name: 'customerLocation', type: 'string'},
                {name: 'isNewOrder', type: 'boolean', defaultValue: true}
        ],
        hasMany: {model: 'OrderLine', name: 'orderlines'},
        proxy: {
            type: 'ajax',
            url : 'orders.json',
            reader: {
                type: 'json',
                root: 'orders',
                totalProperty: 'totalRecords',
                successProperty: 'success'
            },
        timeout: 2000,
    listeners: {
            exception:function (proxy, response, operation) {
              //we are offline. Work with the local store
                orderList.bindStore(offlineStore);
                offlineStore.load();
            }
        }
        }
    }
});


//online data store
onlineStore = new Ext.data.Store({
    model: 'Order'
});


//upon data load, store the data in the local store and use
//the same with the list
onlineStore.addListener('load', function (store, records) {
    offlineStore.proxy.clear();
    offlineStore.add(records);
    offlineStore.sync();
    orderList.bindStore(offlineStore);
});


//offline local data store
offlineStore = new Ext.data.Store({
    model: 'Order',
    proxy: {
```

```
            type: 'localstorage',
            id: 'yapps-01'
        }
});

//list showing the list of orders
orderList = new Ext.List({
  title: 'Orders',
    itemTpl: '<tpl for=".">>div>{orderNbr}
    <b>{description}</b></div></tpl>',
    //on click of disclosure, show the order lines
    onItemDisclosure: function(){
      var orderTabPnl = Ext.getCmp('ordertab-pnl-id');
      var orderLinesPnl = Ext.getCmp('orderlines-pnl-id');
      if (Ext.isEmpty(orderLinesPnl))
        orderLinesPnl = new Ext.List({
        id: 'orderlines-pnl-id',
      title: 'Order Lines',
        itemTpl: '<tpl for=".">>div>{lineNo} - {product}
        <b>{orderedQty}</b></div></tpl>',
        store: new Ext.data.Store({
          model: 'OrderLine',
          data : arguments[0].data.orderlines
      }),
        floating      : true,
        width         : 350,
        height        : 370,
        centered      : true,
        modal         : true,
        hideOnMaskTap: false
    });

    orderTabPnl.add(1, orderLinesPnl);
    orderTabPnl.setActiveItem(1);
    },
    store: onlineStore,
    floating      : true,
    width         : 350,
    height        : 370,
    centered      : true,
    modal         : true,
    hideOnMaskTap: false
});
```

```
var orderTab = new Ext.TabPanel({
id: 'ordertab-pnl-id',
title: 'List',
  fullscreen: true,
  ui        : 'light',
  sortable  : true,
  items: [orderList],
  listeners: {
  //on tab change, remove the order lines panel
    cardswitch: function(tabPnl, newCard, oldCard, index,
      animated) {
      if (index === 0) {
        var orderLinesPnl = Ext.getCmp('orderlines-pnl-id');
        if (!Ext.isEmpty(orderLinesPnl))
          tabPnl.remove(orderLinesPnl);
      }
    }
  }
});

new Ext.TabPanel({
  id: 'tab-pnl-id',
  fullscreen: true,
  ui        : 'light',
  sortable  : true,
  items: [orderTab,
      {
          title: 'Help',
          html: '<h1 style="font-size:16px;"><b>Help</b>
                </h1><p>This application shows the orders and
                  their line items.</p>',
          cls  : 'tab2'
      },
      {
          title: 'About',
          html : '<h1 style="font-size:16px;"><b>About this
                  app!</b></h1><p>Version 0.1</p>',
          cls  : 'tab3'
      }
  ]
});

//load data in the online store
onlineStore.load();
    }
});
```

2. Update the `index.html` file.

3. Deploy and access it from the device of your choice.

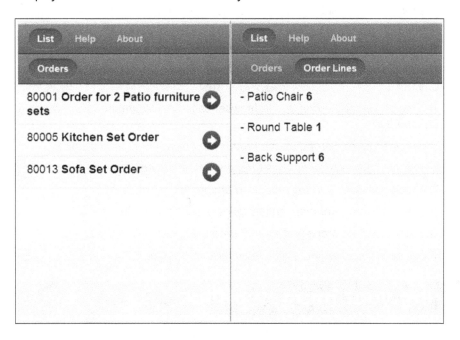

How it works...

In the preceding code, we defined two models: `Order` and `OrderLine`, and the association between them is one-to-many, which is indicated by `hasMany`. Then, we created two stores: `onlineStore` and `offlineStore`. The `onlineStore` is of type `ajax` and loads the order data from the `orders.json` file. The `offlineStore` is bound to the HTML5 localStorage.

`onlineStore` is bound to the `orderList` and we registered a handler for the `load` event on the `onlineStore`. The handler function saves all orders into the local storage and binds the `orderList` to the `offlineStore`. Therefore, we first download all the orders from the remote system, save them locally, and work with the local data.

In order to switch to the offline mode, we used the timeout technique and the exception handler binds `orderList` with the `offlineStore` and loads the data from there.

See also

▶ The recipe named *Setting up the Android-based development environment* in *Chapter 1*

▶ The recipe named *Setting up the iOS-based development environment* in *Chapter 1*

▶ The recipe named *Setting up the Blackberry-based development environment* in *Chapter 1*

▶ The recipe named *Setting up the browser-based development environment* in *Chapter 1*

▶ The recipe named *Setting up the production environment* in *Chapter 1*

▶ The recipe named *Loading data through AJAX using AjaxProxy* in *Chapter 5*

▶ The recipe named *Creating models* in *Chapter 5*

▶ The recipe named *Relating models using association* in *Chapter 5*

▶ The recipe named *Managing a list of data using List* in *Chapter 6*

▶ The recipe named *Working with Tab panels* in *Chapter 6*

Storing your images offline

In the previous recipe, we talked about storing the data offline. Another thing which is used extensively in applications is images, which enhance the overall presentation. Typically, an image is accessed as a URL. These URLs will not be accessible when the device or the browser goes offline. To some extent, this can be managed by using the image-caching feature of the browser and giving it a large expiry time. However, this may not be honored all the time by the browsers. We need a better mechanism to contain the images, which is in complete control of our application. In this recipe, we will see what it takes to persist images locally and use them in the application.

For the demonstration, we will enhance the application that we built in *Chapter 4* where we used the images from a third party website to show the album of flowers, as shown in the following screenshot:

Getting ready

Make sure that you have set up your development environment by following the recipes outlined in *Chapter 1*.

How to do it...

Carry out the following steps:

1. Create and open a new file named `ch08_03.js` and paste the following code into it:

```
Ext.setup({
    onReady: function() {

//Flower model representing a flower record in the data
 Ext.regModel('Flower', {
    fields: [
      'id','album','url','title', 'about'
    ],
```

```
        proxy: {
          type: 'ajax',
          url : 'flowers.json',
          reader: {
              type: 'json',
              root: 'flowers',
              totalProperty: 'totalRecords',
              successProperty: 'success'
          },
          timeout: 2000,
          listeners: {
          exception:function (proxy, response, operation) {
          //we are offline. Use the local storage with the
          //data view
            var dv = Ext.getCmp('dataview-id');
            dv.bindStore(offlineStore);
            offlineStore.load();
          }
      }
        },
    //member method to create the Sencha IO url to get the
    //data url for an image
      setUrl: function() {
        var script = document.createElement("script");
        script.setAttribute("src",
          "http://src.sencha.io/data.setPhotoUrl-" + this.getId() +
          "/" + this.get('url'));
        script.setAttribute("type","text/javascript");
        document.body.appendChild(script);
      }
});

//method to set the data url on a model
setPhotoUrl = function (id, dataUrl) {
      var flower = this.offlineStore.getById(id);
      flower.set('url', dataUrl);
      offlineStore.sync();
  };

//online data store
onlineStore = new Ext.data.Store({
    model: 'Flower'
});
```

```
onlineStore.addListener('load', function (store, records) {
  //after the data is loaded, add them to the local store
  //and bind the local store to the data view
    offlineStore.proxy.clear();
      this.each(function (record) {
          var flower = offlineStore.add(record.data)[0];
          flower.setUrl();
      });
    offlineStore.sync();
    var dv = Ext.getCmp('dataview-id');
    dv.bindStore(offlineStore);
});

//offline data store using the localStorage
offlineStore = new Ext.data.Store({
    model: 'Flower',
    proxy: {
        type: 'localstorage',
        id: 'yapps-02'
    }
});

//template to show the photos
var tpl = new Ext.XTemplate(
    '<tpl for=".">',
      '<div class="thumb-wrap" id="{title}">',
        '<div class="thumb"><img src="{url}"
              title="{title}"></div>',
        '<span>{about}</span></div>',
    '</tpl>',
    '<div class="x-clear"></div>'
);


var filter = function(criteria) {
var dv = Ext.getCmp('dataview-id');
var store = dv.getStore();
return store.filterBy(function(record, id){
  if (record.get('album') === criteria ||
          Ext.isEmpty(criteria))
    return true;
  else
    return false;
  });
```

```
        }


var pnl = new Ext.Panel({
  id:'images-view',
    fullscreen: true,
    scroll: false,
    monitorOrientation: true,
    layout: 'card',
    defaults: {
        border: false
    },
    items: [new Ext.DataView({
        id: 'dataview-id',
        store: onlineStore,
        scroll: 'vertical',
        tpl: tpl,
        autoHeight:true,
        singleSelect: true,
        overItemCls:'x-view-over',
        itemSelector:'div.thumb-wrap',
        emptyText: 'No images to display',
        monitorOrientation: true,
        listeners: {
          selectionchange: function(model, recs) {
            if (recs.length > 0) {
              Ext.getCmp('detail-panel').update('<img
                src="' + recs[0].data.url + '" title="' +
                recs[0].data.title + '">');
              Ext.getCmp('images-
                view').getLayout().setActiveItem(1);
              Ext.getCmp('back-button').show();
              Ext.getCmp('rose-button').hide();
              Ext.getCmp('daffodil-button').hide();
              Ext.getCmp('hibiscus-button').hide();
              }
          },
          orientationchange: function(pnl, orientation,
            width, height){
            pnl.refresh();
          }
        }
      }), new Ext.Panel({
        id: 'detail-panel',
          width: 400,
```

```
                     height: 300,
                     styleHtmlContent: true,
                     scroll: 'vertical',
                     cls: 'htmlcontent'
                })],
        dockedItems: [
          {
             xtype: 'toolbar',
             dock: 'top',
             items: [
                {
                   text: 'Rose',
                   id: 'rose-button',
                   handler: function() {
                      filter('rose');
                   }
                },
                {
                   text: 'Daffodil',
                   id: 'daffodil-button',
                   handler: function() {
                      filter('daffodil');
                   }
                },
                {
                   text: 'Hibiscus',
                   id: 'hibiscus-button',
                   handler: function() {
                      filter('hibiscus');
                   }
                },
                {
                   text: 'Reset',
                   id: 'reset-button',
                   ui: 'decline-round',
                   handler: function() {
                      Ext.getCmp('images-
                         view').getLayout().setActiveItem(0);
                      filter('');
                   }
                }, {
                   text: 'Back',
                   id: 'back-button',
                   ui: 'back',
```

```
              hidden: true,
              handler: function() {
                Ext.getCmp('images-
                  view').getLayout().setActiveItem(0);
                this.hide();
                Ext.getCmp('rose-button').show();
                Ext.getCmp('daffodil-button').show();
                Ext.getCmp('hibiscus-button').show();
              }
            }
          ]
        }
      ]
    });

    onlineStore.load();

  }
});
```

2. Create and open a new file named `flowers.json` in the www folder and paste the following into it:

```
{
"totalRecords" : "20",
"success" : "true",
"flowers": [{
        "id": "1",
        "album":"rose",
        "url":"http://www.pictures.vg/vgflowers/400x300/
          flowers_pics_4870.jpg",
        "title":"Rose 1",
        "about":"Peach"}, {
        "id": "2",
        "album":"rose",
        "url":"http://www.pictures.vg/vgflowers/400x300/
          redroses08.jpg",
        "title":"Rose 2",
        "about":"Red"}, {
        "id": "3",
        "album":"rose",
        "url":"http://www.pictures.vg/vgflowers/400x300/
          abflowers5613.jpg",
        "title":"Rose 3",
        "about":"Pink"}, {
        "id": "4",
```

```
"album":"rose",
"url":"http://www.pictures.vg/vgflowers/400x300/
  cflowers0399.jpg",
"title":"Rose 4",
"about":"Orange"}, {
"id": "5",
"album":"daffodil",
"url":"http://www.pictures.vg/vgflowers/400x300/
  daff001.jpg",
"title":"Daffodil 1",
"about":"Yellow"}, {
"id": "6",
"album":"daffodil",
"url":"http://www.pictures.vg/vgflowers/400x300/
  cflowers0484.jpg",
"title":"Daffodil 2",
"about":"Small"}, {
"id": "7",
"album":"daffodil",
"url":"http://www.pictures.vg/vgflowers/400x300/
  abflowers2232.jpg",
"title":"Daffodil 2",
"about":"Orange"}, {
"id": "8",
"album":"daffodil",
"url":"http://www.pictures.vg/vgflowers/400x300/
  abflowers7230.jpg",
"title":"Daffodil 2",
"about":"Winter"}, {
"id": "9",
"album":"hibiscus",
"url":"http://www.pictures.vg/vgflowers/400x300/
  cflowers4214.jpg",
"title":"Hibiscus 1",
"about":"Peach"}, {
"id": "10",
"album":"hibiscus",
"url":"http://www.pictures.vg/vgflowers/400x300/
  cflowers3250.jpg",
"title":"Hibiscus 1",
"about":"Red"}, {
"id": "11",
"album":"hibiscus",
"url":"http://www.pictures.vg/vgflowers/400x300/
  cflowers2631.jpg",
```

```
      "title":"Hibiscus 1",
      "about":"Pink"}, {
      "id": "12",
      "album":"hibiscus",
      "url":"http://www.pictures.vg/vgflowers/400x300/
        cflowers5645.jpg",
      "title":"Hibiscus 1",
      "about":"Maroon"}, {
      "id": "13",
      "album":"hibiscus",
      "url":"http://www.pictures.vg/vgflowers/400x300/
        cflowers0577.jpg",
      "title":"Hibiscus 1",
      "about":"Pink"}, {
      "id": "14",
      "album":"hibiscus",
      "url":"http://www.pictures.vg/vgflowers/400x300/
        cflowers3224.jpg",
      "title":"Hibiscus 1",
      "about":"Bright Red"
  }]
}
```

3. Create and open a new file named `ch08.css` and paste the following code into it:

```css
#images-view .x-panel-body{
  background: white;
  font: 11px Arial, Helvetica, sans-serif;
}
#images-view .thumb{
  background: #dddddd;
  padding: 3px;
}
#images-view .thumb img{
  height: 60px;
  width: 80px;
}
#images-view .thumb-wrap{
  float: left;
  margin: 4px;
  margin-right: 0;
  padding: 5px;
}
#images-view .thumb-wrap span{
  display: block;
  overflow: hidden;
```

```
      text-align: center;
    }

    #images-view .x-view-over{
      border:1px solid #dddddd;
      background: #efefef url(images/row-over.gif) repeat-x left top;
      padding: 4px;
    }

    #images-view .x-item-selected{
      background: #eff5fb url(images/selected.gif) no-repeat
        right bottom;
      border:1px solid #99bbe8;
      padding: 4px;
    }
    #images-view .x-item-selected .thumb{
      background:transparent;
    }
```

4. Update the `index.html` file.
5. Deploy and access it from the device of your choice.

How it works...

In the preceding code, we defined a model `Flower`. Then, we created two stores: `onlineStore` and `offlineStore`. `onlineStore` is of type `ajax` and loads the order data from the `flowers.json` file. `offlineStore` is bound to the HTML5 localStorage.

`onlineStore` is bound to the data view and we registered a handler for the `load` event on the `onlineStore`. The handler function saves all the orders into the local storage and binds the data view to the `offlineStore`. While adding a model to the local storage, we called the `setUrl` method on the model to set the Sencha IO cloud service to get `dataUrl` corresponding to an image URL. Another alternative to using Sencha IO is to have our own server-side implementation which can convert an image URL to a data URL. After the image is loaded, `id` and `dataUrl` are passed to the `setPhotoUrl` callback method. The callback method then sets the URL on a model to `dataUrl` received from the Sencha IO service and updates the model in the local storage. The `dataUrl` mechanism allows us to persist the image locally without worrying about the browser caching, the expiry time, and so on.

In order to switch to the offline mode, we used the timeout technique and the `exception` handler binds the data view with `offlineStore` and loads the data from there.

 You may learn more about Sencha IO at the following URLs:

`http://www.sencha.com/products/io/`

`http://www.sencha.com/learn/how-to-use-src-sencha-io/`

See also

▸ The recipe named *Setting up the Android-based development environment* in *Chapter 1*

▸ The recipe named *Setting up the iOS-based development environment* in *Chapter 1*

▸ The recipe named *Setting up the Blackberry-based development environment* in *Chapter 1*

▸ The recipe named *Setting up the browser-based development environment* in *Chapter 1*

▸ The recipe named *Setting up the production environment* in *Chapter 1*

▸ The recipe named *Loading data through AJAX using AjaxProxy* in *Chapter 5*

▸ The recipe named *Creating models* in *Chapter 5*

▸ The recipe named *Designing a custom view using DataView* in *Chapter 1*

▸ The recipe named *Using XTemplate for advanced templating* in *Chapter 4*

▸ The recipe named *Storing your data offline* in this chapter

Application caching

So far, we have seen how to detect the online/offline mode and store the data and images locally. The last thing left is to cache the application code, so that they are downloaded locally and are available for offline use. In this recipe, we will go through the steps to achieve it.

Getting ready

Make sure that you have set up your development environment by following the recipes outlined in *Chapter 1*.

How to do it...

Carry out the following steps:

1. Create and open a new file named `touch.manifest` and paste the following code into it:

```
CACHE MANIFEST

#version 0.14

index.html

touch-charts/sencha-touch.js
touch-charts/resources/css/sencha-touch.css

ch08/ch08.css
ch08/ch08_01.js
```

2. Modify the `index.html` file to include the manifest file as follows:

```
<html manifest="touch.manifest">
```

3. Add the following to the `mime.types` file of Apache Web Server:

```
text/cache-manifest          manifest
```

4. Deploy and access it from the device of your choice.

How it works...

The steps outlined use the Cache Manifest to instruct the browser to cache the resources listed in the `touch.manifest` file. To the manifest file, we added a `#version` line, which we update whenever we make any changes to the code. This is added to overcome the problem of resource (JavaScript files) not being reloaded if there are no changes in the manifest file. Afterwards, we added a new MIME type support to our Apache Web Server by extending the `mime.types` file. You may have to check the specifics related to your web server and configure the MIME type accordingly.

Once the manifest file is created and the support is added to the web server, we added the manifest attribute to the `<html>` tag where we specified our manifest file. In this way, the browser will load the manifest file and all the resources listed inside it.

See also

▶ The recipe named *Setting up the Android-based development environment* in *Chapter 1*

▶ The recipe named *Setting up the iOS-based development environment* in *Chapter 1*

▶ The recipe named *Setting up the Blackberry-based development environment* in *Chapter 1*

▶ The recipe named *Setting up the browser-based development environment* in *Chapter 1*

▶ The recipe named *Setting up the production environment* in *Chapter 1*

9

Engaging Users by Responding to Events

In this chapter, we will cover:

- ▶ Handling Touch Events
- ▶ Handling Scroll Events
- ▶ Handling Tap Events
- ▶ Handling Double Tap Events
- ▶ Handling TapHold Events
- ▶ Handling Swipe Events
- ▶ Handling Pinch Events
- ▶ Handling Drag Events

Introduction

Key to building the interactive and responsive UI is event handling. The greater the number of events available, the better the interaction between the user and the application. For example, if we are dragging an element on the screen and if the underlying platform happens to only raise two events—one at the beginning of the drag and one at the end of the drag—then we only get two chances to interact with the element and use the corresponding handlers to respond to those events. However, imagine if the platform also raises the event while the element is on the move. In this way, we can also show the trajectory to the user to show how the element is moving from the starting point to the end point.

So far in different chapters, we have looked at different events raised by the components and we handled some of them. When a web application is used on the touch device, it typically interprets the mouse events to provide the required interactivity. This may put limitations on the user experience as these events are normalized across different devices, and may not utilize the events being offered by the touch device. Additionally, it is not possible to handle the concurrent input even if the device offers multiple touch points. In this chapter, our focus will be on the touch specific events. We will see what are the touch specific events raised by the framework and how can we handle them to respond. The framework implements the Touch Events specification defined by the W3 Consortium. For more details, you may refer to `http://www.w3.org/TR/touch-events`.

Handling Touch Events

This recipe talks about four touch specific events: `touchstart`, `touchdown`, `touchmove`, and `touchend` and also explains how to handle them.

Getting ready

Make sure that you have set up your development environment by following the recipes outlined in *Chapter 1*.

Create a new folder named `ch09` in the same folder where we created the `ch01` and `ch02` folders. We will be using this new folder in which to keep the code.

How to do it...

Carry out the following steps:

1. Create and open a new file named `ch09_01.js` and paste the following code into it:

```
Ext.setup({
    onReady: function() {

    this.handleEvent = function(e) {
      console.log(e.type);
    }


  var pnl = new Ext.Panel({
    id:'main-panel',
      fullscreen: true,
      monitorOrientation: true,
      layout: 'fit',
```

```
          defaults: {
              border: false
          }
      });

      var touchPnl = Ext.getCmp('main-panel');
      touchPnl.mon(touchPnl.el, {
                touchstart: this.handleEvent,
                touchend: this.handleEvent,
                touchmove: this.handleEvent,
                touchdown: this.handleEvent,
                scope: this
            });

      }
  });
```

2. Update the `index.html` file.

3. Deploy and access it from the device of your choice.

Handling Scroll Events

When the scrolling is enabled on a component in Sencha Touch, the framework fires the scroll related events that we use to scroll the content. This recipe lists out the scroll related events and shows how to handle them.

Getting ready

Make sure that you have set up your development environment by following the recipes outlined in _Chapter 1_.

How to do it...

Carry out the following steps:

1. Add the following handler functions inside the `Ext.onReady` in `ch09_01.js`:

```
this.handleScrollEvent = function(e) {
  console.log('scroll');
}

this.handleScrollstartEvent = function(e) {
  console.log('scrollstart');
}
```

```
this.handleScrollendEvent = function(e) {
  console.log('scrollend');
}
```

2. Set `scroll: 'vertical'` property to the panel initialization:

```
var pnl = new Ext.Panel({
  id:'main-panel',
    fullscreen: true,
  scroll: 'vertical',
    monitorOrientation: true,
```

3. Add the following code after the component reference is retrieved using the `Ext.getCmp` method:

```
touchPnl.scroller.mon('scrollstart',this.
  handleScrollstartEvent);
touchPnl.scroller.mon('scroll',this.handleScrollEvent);
touchPnl.scroller.mon('scrollend',this.handleScrollendEvent);
```

4. Deploy and access it from the device of your choice.

Handling Tap Events

This recipe shows the available tap events and ways to handle them.

Getting ready

Make sure that you have set up your development environment by following the recipes outlined in *Chapter 1*.

How to do it...

Carry out the following steps:

1. Add the following events and their handlers to the list of events that we had added on the panel element in the first recipe:

```
singletap: this.handleEvent,
tap: this.handleEvent,
```

2. Deploy and access it from the device of your choice.

Handling Double Tap Events

Similar to double-click on the desktop, there is a `doubletap` event available which can be used to show more details about the tapped element. This recipe shows the event and ways to handle it.

Getting ready

Make sure that you have set up your development environment by following the recipes outlined in *Chapter 1*.

How to do it...

Carry out the following steps:

1. Add the following code after the component reference is retrieved using the `Ext.getCmp` method:

   ```
   doubletap: this.handleEvent,
   ```

2. Deploy and access it from the device of your choice.

Handling TapHold Events

On the touch devices, users can tap and hold their finger in that position. This fires a specific event named `taphold`. This recipe shows how to handle this event. We may use this to enable the dragging of the item. While working with the column charts, we saw how this event is handled to provide the gesture, which allows us to switch between the stacked and grouped modes of the chart.

Getting ready

Make sure that you have set up your development environment by following the recipes outlined in *Chapter 1*.

How to do it...

Carry out the following steps:

1. Add the following events and their handlers to the list of events that we had added on the panel element in the first recipe:

   ```
   taphold: this.handleEvent,
   tapcancel: this.handleEvent,
   ```

2. Deploy and access it from the device of your choice.

Handling Swipe Events

Touch devices are sensitive enough to differentiate between swipe and drag and they raise different events to indicate each of these actions. Here we will see what event is raised in the case of swipe and how we handle it.

Getting ready

Make sure that you have set up your development environment by following the recipes outlined in *Chapter 1*.

How to do it...

Carry out the following steps:

1. Add the following code after the component reference is retrieved using the `Ext.getCmp` method:

   ```
   swipe: this.handleEvent,
   ```

2. Deploy and access it from the device of your choice.

Handling Pinch Events

Pinch is an interesting user action available on touch screens. A user can typically maximize or minimize the content/image using pinch events. There are a different set of pinch events which the Sencha Touch framework provides that we can use to implement some really great interaction. Here we will look at the available list of events related to pinch and how to handle them.

Getting ready

Make sure that you have set up your development environment by following the recipes outlined in *Chapter 1*.

How to do it...

Carry out the following steps:

1. Add the following code after the component reference is retrieved using the `Ext.getCmp` method:

   ```
   pinch: this.handleEvent,
   pinchstart: this.handleEvent,
   pinchend: this.handleEvent,
   ```

2. Deploy and access it from the device of your choice.

Handling Drag Events

When an element is dragged on the screen, the framework gives us different events to indicate that the drag has started, the item is on the move, and the drag has ended. In this recipe, we will look at the drag specific events.

Getting ready

Make sure that you have set up your development environment by following the recipes outlined in *Chapter 1*.

How to do it...

Carry out the following steps:

1. Add the following code after the component reference is retrieved using the `Ext.getCmp` method:

   ```
   dragstart: this.handleEvent,
   drag: this.handleEvent,
   dragend: this.handleEvent,
   ```

2. Deploy and access it from the device of your choice.

10
Increased Relevance Using Geolocation

In this chapter, we will cover:

- ▶ Finding out your location
- ▶ Auto update of your location
- ▶ Tracking direction and speed
- ▶ Hooking up Google Maps with your application
- ▶ Working with the Google Maps options
- ▶ Mapping Geolocation on Google Maps

Introduction

Imagine how good it would be to build an application which can automatically determine the user mobile location and provide local searches such as suggests places of interest, hotels, nearest police station, and so on. Imagine how the user would feel if, after determining their location, we display the relevant information and the routes on a map, which gives clear directions on how to reach a place. Another example could be providing an application which can tell my average speed while I am jogging or an application which can help track the fleet of trucks, provide a route map which is less congested, send an SOS message to a friend with my location details, and so on.

All of this is feasible and possible with the newly introduced Geolocation specification from the W3 Consortium (http://dev.w3.org/geo/api/spec-source.html).

This specification provides us the required objects, methods, and events to get the location detail and work with it.

In this chapter, we will look at the classes provided by the Sencha Touch framework to work with Geolocation. The classes implement the W3C Geolocation specification. Additionally, we will see how to work with Google Maps and complement it with Geolocation.

Sencha Touch wraps Google Maps Javascript APIs, outlined in `http://code.google.com/apis/maps/documentation/javascript/`, into a convenient class, which we will be making use of in this chapter.

Finding out your location

W3C's Geolocation specification is implemented by the `Ext.util.GeoLocation` class in Sencha Touch. In this recipe, we will look into the class and see how to learn about our device location.

Getting ready

Make sure that you have set up your development environment by following the recipes outlined in *Chapter 1*.

Create a new folder named `ch10` in the same folder where we had created the `ch01` and `ch02` folders. We will be using this new folder in which to keep the code.

How to do it...

Carry out the following steps:

1. Create and open a new file named `ch10_01.js` and paste the following code into it:

```
Ext.setup({
    onReady: function() {


    var geo = new Ext.util.GeoLocation({
        autoUpdate: false,
        listeners: {
            locationupdate: function (geo) {
                alert('New latitude: ' + geo.latitude + ' : longitude : '
                    + geo.longitude + ' @ ' + geo.timestamp);
            },
            locationerror: function (   geo,
                    bTimeout,
                    bPermissionDenied,
                    bLocationUnavailable,
                    message) {
                        if(bTimeout){
```

```
                        alert('Timeout occurred.');
                    }
                    if (bPermissionDenied){
                        alert('Permission denied.');
                    }
                    if (bLocationUnavailable) {
                      alert('Location unavailable.');
                    }
                }
            }
        });

    geo.updateLocation();


    }
});
```

2. Update the `index.html` file.

3. Deploy and access it from the device of your choice. You will see a message showing the longitude and latitude of your location, as shown in the following screenshot:

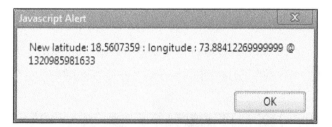

How it works...

In the preceding code, we created an instance of the `Ext.util.GeoLocation` class with `autoUpdate` set to `false`. This means that the browser will not watch for a change in location. The update is fired manually by calling the `updateLocation` method on the `geo` object. Additionally, on the `geo` object, listeners have been set up for the `locationupdate` and `locationerror` events. The `locationupdate` event is fired when the location is updated. The framework passes the object representing the location information at that instance in time. The `geo` object contains the following fields:

▸ `latitude`
▸ `longitude`

- ▶ timestamp
- ▶ accuracy
- ▶ altitude
- ▶ altitudeAccuracy
- ▶ heading
- ▶ speed

Out of the preceding listed properties, latitude, longitude, timestamp, and accuracy will be provided. However, other properties can be null based on the device on which we are using the API.

If any errors occur while trying to get the updated location information, the framework fires the locationerror event where it indicates the following three types of errors:

1. The operation timed-out
2. User does not have permission
3. Location information is not available

See also

- ▶ The recipe named *Setting up the Android-based development environment* in *Chapter 1*
- ▶ The recipe named *Setting up the iOS based-development environment* in *Chapter 1*
- ▶ The recipe named *Setting up the Blackberry-based development environment* in *Chapter 1*

Auto-update of your location

In some applications, manual updating of location may not be desirable, for example, if your application is expected to update the location periodically to show the path in which a vehicle is moving. In this recipe, we will see how to configure the Ext.util.GeoLocation class to have the location automatically updated and how to control the frequency with which the location update should be attempted.

Getting ready

Make sure that you have set up your development environment by following the recipes outlined in *Chapter 1*.

How to do it...

Carry out the following steps;

1. Set the following properties on the `Ext.util.GeoLocation` class while instantiating:

   ```
   autoUpdate: true,
   timeout: 5000,  //5 sec
   ```

2. Deploy and access it from the device of your choice.

How it works...

Setting `autoUpdate` to `true` no longer requires the application code to call the `updateLocation` method, explicitly. The location is updated automatically and the `locationupdate` or `locationerror` event is fired based on whether the update operation was successful or not.

The `timeout` property allows us to control how frequently the location update will be attempted. It accepts the time in milliseconds, for example, in the preceding code snippet, we set the value to 5000 milliseconds (5 sec). This is a useful property if you want to save your mobile's battery, as frequent updates will eat it up.

See also

▸ The recipe named Setting up the *Android-based development environment* in *Chapter 1*

▸ The recipe named *Setting up the iOS-based development environment* in *Chapter 1*

▸ The recipe named *Setting up Blackberry-based development environment* in *Chapter 1*

▸ The recipe named *Finding out your location* in this chapter

Tracking direction and speed

The `GeoLocation` object in Sencha Touch provides properties which we can use to figure out the direction and the speed at which we are moving. This could be useful in applications where you may want to suggest to the user the nearest petrol pump based on his direction. In this recipe, we will look at the use of related properties.

Getting ready

Make sure that you have set up your development environment by following the recipes outlined in *Chapter 1*.

How to do it...

Carry out the following steps:

1. In the `locationupdate` event handler, add the following line of code:

    ```
    alert('Heading: ' + geo.heading + ': Speed:' + geo.speed);
    ```

2. Deploy and access it from the device of your choice.

How it works...

The preceding code uses the two important properties of the `GeoLocation` class: `heading` and `speed`. The `heading` property gives the direction of the travel of the device. It is specified in non-negative degrees between 0 and 359. The angle is returned with respect to the real North. If the device is stationary, the value of this property is `undefined`.

The `speed` property gives the current ground speed of the device and the value will be in meters per second. If the device is stationary, the value of this property is 0.

These two properties are optional and may not be available on every device. If these properties are not supported on a device, their value will be `null`. For example, on Android, the values returned are `null`. On such devices, we can derive these values using the `longitude`, `latitude`, and `timestamp`.

See also

- ▶ The recipe named *Setting up the Android-based development environment* in *Chapter 1*
- ▶ The recipe named *Setting up the iOS-based development environment in Chapter 1*
- ▶ The recipe named Setting *up the Blackberry-based development environment* in *Chapter 1*
- ▶ The recipe named *Finding out your location* in this chapter

Hooking up Google Maps with your application

Google provides the map service and also the APIs to integrate it into our application. Sencha Touch has wrapped it inside a component named Ext.util.Map, which provides the complete map related functionality. It uses Google Maps' JavaScript APIs, internally, to provide us a working map component. In this recipe, we will see how to make use of the Map class.

Getting ready

Make sure that you have set up your development environment by following the recipes outlined in *Chapter 1*.

How to do it...

Carry out the following steps:

1. Create and open a new file named ch10_02.js and paste the following code into it:

```
Ext.setup({
    onReady: function() {

    var pnl = new Ext.Panel({
        fullscreen: true,
        items      : [
            {
                xtype : 'map'

            }
        ]
    });

    }
});
```

2. Update the index.html file.

3. Add the following to the index.html file to include Google Maps, JavaScript APIs:

```
<script type="text/javascript" src="http://maps.google.com/maps/
api/js?sensor=true"></script>
```

4. Deploy and access it from the device of your choice. You will see a screen showing Google Maps with its default longitude and latitude set to Palo Alto, as shown in the following screenshot:

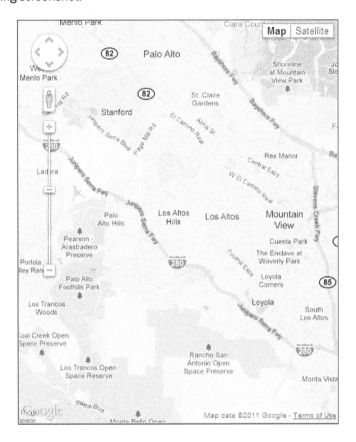

How it works...

In the preceding code, we created a panel and added a map component to it using the `xtype: 'map'`. Usage of this `xtype` leads to the instantiation of the `Ext.util.Map` class, which wraps Google Maps inside it. It initializes the Google Maps class with the following default map options:

▶ Map center is set to the location of Palo Alto (latitude—37.381592, longitude—122.135672)

▶ Map type is set to ROADMAP

▶ Zoom level is set to 12

- ▶ The recipe named *Setting up the Android-based development environment* in *Chapter 1*

- ▶ The recipe named *Setting up the iOS-based development environment* in *Chapter 1*

- ▶ The recipe named *Setting up the Blackberry-based development environment* in *Chapter 1*

Working with Google Maps options

In the previous recipe, we looked at the default map options set by the `Ext.util.Map` class. In your application, say you are building an application to show forest, mountains, and rivers around a particular place. In this case, you will have to set the map options according to your application need. This recipe will show us how to achieve this.

Getting ready

Make sure that you have set up your development environment by following the recipes outlined in *Chapter 1*.

How to do it...

Carry out the following steps:

1. Edit the `ch10_02.js` file and add the `mapOptions` property as shown in the following code:

```
Ext.setup({
    onReady: function() {

  var pnl = new Ext.Panel({
    fullscreen: true,
    items     : [
        {
            xtype : 'map',
            mapOptions: {
              center: new google.maps.LatLng(17.22, 78.28),
              mapTypeId: google.maps.MapTypeId.TERRAIN,
              zoom: 10
            }
        }
    ]
});
    }
});
```

2. Deploy and access it from the device of your choice. You will see a screen showing Google Maps with its default longitude and latitude set to 78.28 and 17.22, respectively, as shown in the following screenshot:

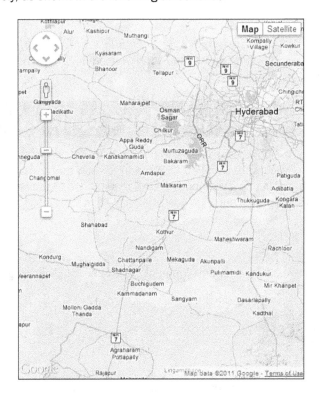

How it works...

In the preceding code, we set the `mapOptions` property on the `Ext.util.Map` class, which accepts the `mapOptions` config that the Google Maps API can take. We specified three properties: `center`, `mapTypeId`, and `zoom`. To the `center` property, we set the latitude and longitude of a location that will be used to center the map. The longitude and latitude specified here are of Hyderabad, India. The `mapTypeId` property is set to `TERRAIN`, so that in our application we can show mountains, forest, and rivers around the center location. Using `zoom` we set the map zoom level to 10.

▶ The recipe named *Setting up the Android-based development environment* in *Chapter 1*

▶ The recipe named *Setting up the iOS-based development environment* in *Chapter 1*

▶ The recipe named *Setting up the Blackberry-based development environment* in *Chapter 1*

▶ The recipe named *Hooking up Google Maps with your application* in this chapter

Mapping Geolocation on Google Maps

So far in this chapter, we have looked at the `Ext.util.GeoLocation` and `Ext.util.Map` classes of Sencha Touch to see how to get the location and how to display a map. In this recipe, we will put these two pieces together, so that the location information from the `GeoLocation` class can be used on the `Map` class in rendering the information on the map. This can then be used, for example, to highlight the nearest restaurants on the map, based on the current location.

Getting ready

Make sure that you have set up your development environment by following the recipes outlined in *Chapter 1*.

How to do it...

Carry out the following steps:

1. Create and open a new file named `ch10_03.js` and paste the following code into it:

```
Ext.setup({
    onReady: function() {

        var geo = new Ext.util.GeoLocation({
            autoUpdate: true,
            listeners: {
                locationupdate: function (geo) {
                    var map = Ext.getCmp('google-map-id');
                    map.update(geo);
                },
                locationerror: function (   geo,
                    bTimeout,
                    bPermissionDenied,
                    bLocationUnavailable,
```

```
                    message) {
                       if(bTimeout){
                            alert('Timeout occurred.');
                       }
                       if (bPermissionDenied){
                            alert('Permission denied.');
                       }
                       if (bLocationUnavailable) {
                         alert('Location unavailable.');
                       }
                   }
               }
       });

       var pnl = new Ext.Panel({
          fullscreen: true,
          items    : [
              {
                  xtype: 'map',
                  id: 'google-map-id',
                  geo: geo,
                  mapOptions: {
                    mapTypeId: google.maps.MapTypeId.TERRAIN,
                    zoom: 10
                  }
              }
          ]
       });

       }
   });
```

2. Update the `index.html` file.

3. Deploy and access it from the device of your choice. You will see a screen showing a Google map with the location set as per the longitude and latitude values returned by the Geolocation API, as shown in the following screenshot:

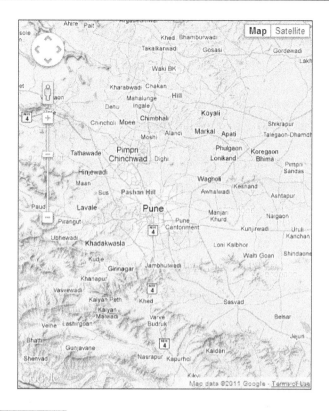

How it works...

In the preceding code, we created the `GeoLocation` instance with `autoUpdate` set to `true` and also a panel with a map. We have given an ID to the map component—`google-map-id`—which we use in the `locationupdate` event listener on the `GeoLocation` object. This then gets the map component and calls the `update` method on it to update the map with the new location information. Though the complete `geo` object is passed to the `update` method, it only uses the `longitude` and `latitude` properties of it. This way the location information fetched from the `GeoLocation` is passed on to the `Map` to get them working together.

See also

- ▸ The recipe named *Setting up the Android-based development environment* in *Chapter 1*

- ▸ The recipe named *Setting up the iOS-based development environment* in *Chapter 1*

- ▸ The recipe named *Setting up the Blackberry-based development environment* in *Chapter 1*

- ▸ The recipe named *Finding out your location* in this chapter

- ▸ The recipe named *Hooking up Google Maps with your application* in this chapter

Index

Thank you for buying
Sencha Touch Cookbook

About Packt Publishing

Packt, pronounced 'packed', published its first book "*Mastering phpMyAdmin for Effective MySQL Management*" in April 2004 and subsequently continued to specialize in publishing highly focused books on specific technologies and solutions.

Our books and publications share the experiences of your fellow IT professionals in adapting and customizing today's systems, applications, and frameworks. Our solution based books give you the knowledge and power to customize the software and technologies you're using to get the job done. Packt books are more specific and less general than the IT books you have seen in the past. Our unique business model allows us to bring you more focused information, giving you more of what you need to know, and less of what you don't.

Packt is a modern, yet unique publishing company, which focuses on producing quality, cutting-edge books for communities of developers, administrators, and newbies alike. For more information, please visit our website: www.packtpub.com.

Writing for Packt

We welcome all inquiries from people who are interested in authoring. Book proposals should be sent to author@packtpub.com. If your book idea is still at an early stage and you would like to discuss it first before writing a formal book proposal, contact us; one of our commissioning editors will get in touch with you.

We're not just looking for published authors; if you have strong technical skills but no writing experience, our experienced editors can help you develop a writing career, or simply get some additional reward for your expertise.

PUBLISHING

Android 3.0 Application Development Cookbook

ISBN: 978-1-84951-294-7   Paperback: 272 pages

Over 70 working recipes covering every aspect of Android development

1. Written for Android 3.0 but also applicable to lower versions

2. Quickly develop applications that take advantage of the very latest mobile technologies, including web apps, sensors, and touch screens

3. Part of Packt's Cookbook series: Discover tips and tricks for varied and imaginative uses of the latest Android features

jQuery Mobile First Look

ISBN: 978-1-84951-590-0   Paperback: 216 pages

Discover the endless possibilities offered by jQuery Mobile for rapid Mobile Web Development

1. Easily create your mobile web applications from scratch with jQuery Mobile

2. Learn the important elements of the framework and mobile web development best practices

3. Customize elements and widgets to match your desired style

4. Step-by-step instructions on how to use jQuery Mobile

Please check **www.PacktPub.com** for information on our titles